S0-DOO-413

THE Tattered Quilt

Grace Dyer

© 2002 by Grace Dyer

ALL RIGHTS RESERVED
This book or parts thereof may not be reproduced
in any form without written permission of the Author.

Published by Word For Word Publishing Co., Inc.
14 MetroTech Center, Brooklyn, NY 11021
(800) 601-WORD
Info@WordForWordPC.com

Printed in Canada

Book cover designed by BYFIELDESIGN
Edited by Michelle A. Edwards

ISBN: 1-889732-30-3

About the Author

Grace Dyer is an evangelist, prophetess, wife, and mother of six children. She and her husband, Rudy minister to young adults in Wyandanch, Long Island, New York. Grace's intense personal experiences during her formative years lend to her ability to effectively minister to the needs of this special population. Although she is a mere 33 years young, Grace was inspired to share her story of God's grace in her life through this spiritual autobiography so that other may find hope in Christ Jesus.

Acknowledgments

I would like to thank my Lord and Savior Jesus Christ. Without Him this work would not have been completed. I also thank the entire Dyer family – my mother, my siblings, and my mentor, Prophetess Sharon Page. I thank the Lord for using you to help me give birth to my prophetic ministry in the office of the prophetess. Thanks also to my friends Chante and L.J. Logan, and Stephanie and Rodney Burke. Thank you so much Cheryl Krugman - of AIL; I really appreciate you giving me the loan for this book when so many people wouldn't. Thanks a million!

To the Dowling family, thanks for being there for me. In loving memory of Ann Dowling. I love you!

To my prayer group, thanks so much for your prayers.

Thank you Dee for the typewriter. It was truly a God send and so are you.

To my beautiful children: I thank you for your inspiration.

To my sisters and partners in ministry: prophetess Kim Ferguson and Evangelist

Tanya Hooks, I am looking forward to winning souls for Jesus with you!

Candy Inez Stewart: Thank you for being my protection for your humor and most of all my friend in my darkest hours.

El Keisha and LaKema. Thank you for your prayers. I'm glad to see you on the Master's side.

To my wonderful husband Rudy, words cannot describe your love for me and mine for you. You are a <u>true</u> man of God. Thank you for accepting me just the way I am. You were the one who told me, "don't think you can, but know you can!" Your support has been invaluable.

To my book cover artist, Eric Roberson, thank you for your awesome work. "Is the world ready for you?"

Many thanks to Word For Word Publishing Co. and its team; Carolyn Davis, you sincerely believed this story should be told. I love ya! Thank you Michelle Edwards, my super editor, who helped me get it all on paper. Thank you so much Janice Dixon for your editorial assistance.

*This book is dedicated to all
the "Tattered Quilts."*

TABLE OF CONTENTS

Introduction

As I laid upon my bed thinking of a title for this autobiography, I said "Lord, what will be the name You choose?" I got an image of Joseph and how his father, Jacob, loved him so much. He blessed Joseph with a coat of many colors. Joseph wore that coat with pride. It symbolized his father's love for him.

Joseph had special dreams that he shared with his brothers, and his brothers were angered by the dreams. But the coat their father gave Joseph angered them more. His brothers smeared animal's blood on it and returned the coat to their father. Even though Jacob didn't see his son, he saw the coat and the condition of the coat and it broke his heart.

The Lord has given me a quilt in a spiritual sense. A quilt can be passed down from generation to generation. It symbolizes my life and my heavenly Father's love for me. It's been used, worn, and stained, but not destroyed. That's me, I've been torn but I am *not destroyed!* The interweaving of God's grace has strengthened the fabric of my life. May this story of His grace bless you richly!

The Tattered Quilt

Chapter 1

Ruffled Edges
1968

My sister Monica, who was about eighteen at the time, recalls this event of my birth. She said, "Grace, we didn't even know that our Mom was carrying you because she said she had a tumor." One day my sister went to check on our Mom because she was very sick. When Monica pulled back the covers, there I was. My sister recalls being terrified because she saw lots of blood and me still attached to the umbilical cord covered with placenta. She ran and called 9-1-1. A woman, a friend of the family, I believe, came over. She grabbed me by my feet and pulled out the rest of me. My sister said she remembers yelling, "We need a name. What's her name?" My Mom joined her. They decided to name me after the woman who delivered me, Mrs. Grace. Grace means, "God's gift, unmerited favor."

I was born unto my parents, Sandra Leigh-Jones and Wallace Jake Johnson. My Mom was not to my recognition a saved, fire-baptized woman. She was an alcoholic and my dad, whom I never knew, was one too.

I don't remember having any spiritual dreams, visions, or heavenly visitation from Jesus, angels, or even demons. I didn't know God, nor His supreme existence.

A lot of violence always broke out in the Johnson home. This was no weekend brawl but a Sunday through Saturday cussing, fighting, love making, cussing, more fighting, making love thing every day.

My brothers and sisters described me as a pain in the butt. My sister Monica often pointed out how my voice sounded like a moose. I was a crier and was spoiled according to my big brother. Monica also pointed out how my little brothers and I threw newspapers down the toilet and clogged it; when visitors showed up, we would run out and hide behind the couch. We were very shy kids.

I remember my Dad wanting to be intimate with my Mom and her refusing. That's when the fist fights started. In the midst of this battle, my head was slammed into a radiator.

Somehow, I wound up hurt most of the time. My little brothers and I liked to hang onto our mother's skirt tail and that's part of the reason for my injuries.

One day there was more arguing. This time it was not coming from my parents because my Dad was no longer in the picture. He had been beaten up by my big brothers (as so many other men before him). He had lye thrown on him by my older sisters because of the beating he had given my mother. He threw up his hands and called it quits. This arguing was different. It included my family members, but also strange people. There were police in the apartment and a white lady. They were arguing about something that happened. Could it be because of the blood-soaked bed and the little baby that was laying unconscious on it?

A few days later we were inside a court building. My brothers and I were running around the chairs in the lobby. There was a commotion. We stopped running.

"What is going on?" I asked myself. "No, No," my sister Monica was saying. My Mom was crying and my brothers were cursing and arguing. I came to a standstill, my hands hanging limply at my side. I had the thickest, nappiest hair you ever want to see, and it was in a matted ponytail. I was wearing my favorite red sweater with white boots that covered my calves. What a sight I must have been standing there along with my little brothers who were just as crusty and dusty as I. We just stood there staring. Then that white woman whom I had seen in our apartment came over to us as the police moved my family to another end of the court building to calm them. She gathered us together and knelt down in front of us. She gave us a big smile and began to talk nicely to us. I don't remember what she said, but I do remember her name, Annie Bogan. I liked her right away. It would be many years before I saw my family again.

My brothers and I, the four youngest of the family, were separated. Anthony and Keith were moved to a family in Brooklyn, New York, and Eddie and I were moved to Manhattan. I hated it there. Mrs. Bogan took Eddie and me to our first foster home. I was about four years old, and I was getting pretty excited because I thought I was going to spend time with Mrs. Bogan. She did tell me I would be staying with a family, but I had my own ideas and plans of where and with whom I would be staying. I believed I would be visiting and then returning to my family.

The door opened up and a woman smiled at Eddie and me. She was our new foster Mom. She shook Mrs. Bogan's hand and gestured for us to sit in the living room. The two women engaged in a long conversation. I did not feel interested at all. The woman was a little chunky and brown-skinned, with gray streaks splicing through her short-cropped hair.

I began to wander around because I was always a little curious. In a big room there was a couch, a chair, table, lamps, and lots of pictures on the wall displaying cottages and rivers. Sitting in exquisite glass bowls were candy mints of pinks and greens, walnuts, almonds and peppermints, the kind that are big and round and that melt right away as you suck on them. I began to pack my pockets like a pirate who had found gold treasure.

Then Mrs. Bogan called me over and introduced me to the stern-looking woman. "Grace, come here please honey. This is Mrs. Jenkins. You will be staying with her for a little while, Okay?" I did not want to stay with anyone but Mrs. Bogan. "Now Grace, listen to me, take care of your little brother. Okay? I will see you soon, I promise," Mrs. Bogan continued. She rose and gathered her coat and pocket book. When Mrs. Bogan headed down the hallway toward the front door, I sprinted behind the two women, yelling and babbling something. Mrs. Bogan turned, leaned back, and looked past Mrs. Jenkins. "No honey, you stay here with Mrs. Jenkins. She's going to take care of you," she said. Without turning around, Mrs. Jenkins put out her arm and held me back. "No, no I'm going with you. I'm going with you, or take me back to my family. I don't want to stay here," I screamed. Mrs. Bogan opened the door and exited with the promise that she'd see me soon. She looked sad.

I stopped struggling, enough to see if she would burst the door open and take my brother and me away from that place. Hearing her footsteps going toward the elevator crushed my heart.

When my retaliation resumed, Mrs. Jenkins struck me on my leg. I stopped crying instantly and began to whimper. "Now come with me to the kitchen to get something to eat," Mrs. Jenkins instructed. "Are you hungry?" I was hungry, but I didn't want her to know that, so I remained silent and chose not to follow her.

"Gracie, come on in the kitchen so I can feed you," she called.

She was unaware of my pocket full of nuts and candy. When she was out of my sight or fast asleep, whichever came first, I would feast on my stuff.

"Gracie," she called, sticking her head out from the kitchen doorway. "Come here."

"Nope."

She emerged from the kitchen smiling and headed down the hallway toward me.

I backed up a few inches and shook my head. She hesitated a moment and then advanced toward me again. "Come on, Gracie."

When I backed up, she advanced. We continued this dance for a moment until my back hit the front door knob. She was a few steps away from me.

I turned around quickly and reached for the doorknob. "No! Gracie, No!" The prison warden grabbed my arm. "You come with me so I can feed you." I struggled and yelled until I saw her raise her hand. I remembered the sting of my previous beating.

By then the noise awakened Eddie and he was crying. Mrs. Jenkins pulled me into the kitchen, plopped me down, and pushed a spoon in my hand. "EAT," she snapped and left the kitchen. When she was out of sight, I turned to the meal in front of me. There are tiny bugs on my plate! There was another brown bug crawling on the wall. I screamed. Mrs. Jenkins entered cradling Eddie in her arms, with his bottle dangling in his mouth. "What is it Gracie; why are you yelling?"

I pointed to the bugs on my plate and then to the one that was crawling on the wall.

"What? You don't like black-eye peas and rice?"

I shook my head defiantly. With a swift motion Mrs. Jenkins smashed her shoe against the roach. "Now eat! I'll be back," she ordered, walking out of the room. When she glared over her shoulder at me, I put a heaping mound of rice and bugs in my mouth. Satisfied, Mrs. Jenkins nodded and left.

Instantly, I spat the mess into the plate as my stomach revolted. The wall clock kept an almost silent rhythm. Then finally she returned. "Oh Gracie, you didn't eat your food; now it's all cold! Here let me warm it up."

"No!" I cried.

"What, you're not hungry?"

Hunger was the better of my options. "No," I muttered.

"Okay, let me wash you up and get you ready for bed." As we headed for the bathroom, I glanced back at the murder scene on the wall.

Bath time was my favorite time, so I headed for the tub. I should have known that even bathing wouldn't have been uneventful. Mrs. Jenkins and I fought over my white boots, because I climbed into the tub wearing them. Our pulling back and forth landed my butt on the cold floor and my head thumping against the door.

"I'm sorry, I'm so sorry," Mrs. Jenkins pleaded, "but you wouldn't gimme your foot. I had to grab you like that." She continued to apologize.

I was theatrical, so I milked her remorse for all it was worth. My cries lingered for a while, then I quieted, but not without her paying for the rice and bugs and for stopping my escape. I topped it off by urinating on the floor. That would teach her to mess with a Johnson.

"Gracie!" Mrs. Jenkins yelled. "Why didn't you tell me you had to use the bathroom? Oh, my

God! You done peed all over the floor. I just cleaned this bathroom. Get in the tub child." I carefully put one foot in and slowly brought in the other foot. The water was hot, but Mrs. Jenkins coaxed me to sit in it.

I lowered my body ever so slowly as the hot air rose from the water to my bottom.

"Come on Gracie, sit down now child," she commanded impatiently.

I glared at her. Did she not know how hot the water was?

Mrs. Jenkins took my shoulders and pushed me into the hot, pearly white suds.

When my bottom touched the water, I jerked up an inch and then slowly down another inch or two. I continued the routine slowly until the water covered my lower body.

"Sit down child." Mrs. Jenkins shoved me down. Simultaneously, Eddie's cries rang toward the bathroom door. Mrs. Jenkins deserted me for Eddie. I was left with the soap and rag to finish the job. She had left the bathroom door ajar, so a little cool air seeped into the bathroom. I wiggled my toes and brought them up to surface with soap suds resting on top. This was the only fun I'd had so far. I didn't care if she ever returned. In fact, as soon as I got a chance I would take my baby brother with me and break out of that penitentiary.

Mrs. Jenkins had a daughter, Lisa. Lisa was a lot older than I. She could have been nineteen or in her early twenties, but often she would baby-sit my brother and me while Mrs. Jenkins ran her errands. I didn't like Lisa at all. In fact, I was afraid of her.

"Moth-eaten"

One particular day Mrs. Jenkins went out. Eddie and I were in our little closet of a room when Lisa called me.

I quickly got off the bed and glanced over at Eddie who was sleeping in his crib. He was sleeping with his little butt hunched in the air and his bottle sticking out of his mouth.

"Gracie, Gracie come here," Lisa called out again. "I'm coming, I'm coming," I called back, but not without giving Eddie a quick peck on his forehead.

I walked right across into the room where I knew Lisa would be. The room was dim and a TV was on.

"Come here, Gracie," Lisa patted a spot on her bed right next to her. "Come sit here," she patted the spot again. I climbed up and sat next to her.

"Lie down now," she said, giving me a shove.

I was thinking that it was not bed time yet and I was not sleepy, but I obeyed. Lisa climbed on top of me and began to move slowly, rhythmically. My heart pounded as her breathing moved from slow to a panting sound and her hip movement intensified. I was terrified but I dared not move; I had seen her rage already. Then she stopped and rolled off me still panting. She mounted me again and repeated her motion. Moments later I heard the key in the front door lock. Mrs. Jenkins had been struggling to open the door. Lisa jumped off me. "Get up, go sit at the foot of the bed and act like you're watching TV" she whispered harshly. "You better not tell anyone or I'll beat the mess out of you." She looked at me for a reply. "You hear me?" I nodded my head and turned quickly toward the TV. So many things were going through my mind. Lisa had continued to rape and molest me for quite some time after that.

"Tireless Stitches"

I didn't escape from Mrs. Jenkins' house that day, nor any time soon. In fact, I stayed there for two years. I was about six years old then, and the nice social worker Mrs. Bogan was on her way to pick up Eddie and me. We would go live with the family that took care of my other two brothers,

Anthony and Keith. The woman my brothers lived with stated that she wanted this to take place so we can get to know one another. All the adults had agreed so we had our bags packed and were patiently waiting for Mrs. Bogan to come for us.

Mrs. Bogan did indeed come back to see me just as she had promised. She took us out for lunch and spent time with us. She constantly wrote things down in a notebook. Mrs. Bogan was Jewish. She lived in a very, very clean neighborhood, where people greeted one another with nods and smiles, and where there were fruit stands and sloped sidewalks.

When we got to the house where my two little brothers, Anthony and Keith, were living, I opened the gate and ran up to the front door. I was amazed at how huge the house was; it climbed toward the sky. I was excited and anxious about seeing my brothers so I rang the door bell. "Just a minute," I heard a female voice holler. Mrs. Bogan was paying the cab driver; then she picked up the suitcase that had our clothes. She led Eddie by the hand and was heading our way.

"Yes," the voice said and the door opened. The voice belonged to an older woman. She was wearing a white dress that looked like a nurse's dress, and she had lots of gray hair. Later, I found out it was a wig.

"Hello! What's your name?" she asked.

I smiled back and replied, "My name is Grace and I don't like to be called Gracie. Where are my brothers?!" I demanded.

"Now, Grace," Mrs. Bogan said sharply, "be polite. This is Mrs. Evans."

She shook my hand. "Hello again, Grace, come on in. It is so hot out; do you want something to drink?"

"Yes please," Mrs. Bogan replied.

"Yeah," I said.

"No, the answer is 'Yes,'" Mrs. Evans corrected. "Say yes," she insisted.

I looked at her a moment and obeyed, but in my mind I rebelled.

"Well come on in the living room, sit down and I'll bring you something to drink. And you must be Freddie." She grabbed my brother's hand and played with him. "Hi ya Freddie, how ya doing?"

Eddie babbled in baby talk, he was about one or two then.

"His name is Eddie, not Freddie," I snapped.

"Oh, I'm sorry Eddie," Mrs. Evans said, but not without giving me a warning look. I returned the look before going in search of my brothers. I found them easily.

"Hey! Hi Pumkin, Hi Weiner," I yelled as I ran up and playfully punched them in the arms.

"Hi," they both said. "You want to play with us?"

I snatched a basketball from them and began to bounce the ball in the wide concrete slab on the side of the yard.

"Hey, share the ball," Pumkin yelled. "And don't call me Pumkin anymore. My name's Anthony."

"Yeah, and I'm not Weiner; I am Keith," the other snapped.

"Well, ya'll didn't mind it before. What's the big deal?"

"The big deal is we live here now and everyone calls us by our real names," Anthony explained.

"Pumpkin and Weiner are your real names, dummies."

"No, they're not! They are nicknames and besides we don't use them anymore." Anthony was angry.

"All right dummy," I said. "Calm down."

"I'm not a dummy," Anthony objected.

"Yes, you are."

"No, I'm not!"

"Yes, you are," I continued to tease.

"Hey, Hey," interrupted Mrs. Evans and Mrs. Bogan standing in the back door.

"Grace, come here honey," Mrs. Bogan called. She was holding Eddie. "Gimme a hug. I'm going now and I'll see you in a few weeks. I left my number with Mrs. Evans, if you need me, or if you just want to talk, give me a call."

I had lots to say, but not with Mrs. Evans standing there. "Anthony, Keith, you do the same. Okay?"

"Yes, Mrs. Bogan," they said in unison.

"Now you kids continue to play, I'm walking Mrs. Bogan to the door. I'll be back," my new foster Mom said.

"All right, Grandma," Anthony and Keith said.

Grandma? I said to myself. She's not my Grandma.

A few minutes later Mrs. Evans returned holding Eddie in her arms.

"Now what's going on back here?" she asked.

"Grace called us dummies," Anthony offered up rather quickly.

What a butt kisser! I thought.

Mrs. Evans turned toward me, "Is that true?"

"No! I didn't say it," I answered nonchalantly.

"Yes, you did," Anthony insisted.

"Nope. I didn't."

"Well," Mrs. Evans said as she held up a hand to silence Anthony. "I know what I heard and from what I heard, you did say it. I will not tolerate lying in my house. Now I ask you, did you say it?"

"Nope," I said.

I heard Anthony grunt like a pig. Mrs. Evans quickly put Eddie down and leaped at me. She grabbed my arm in a vice-like grip and pulled me inside. Once inside she pounded my head and back. She was very heavy handed. Eventually, she stopped, almost out of breath.

"Now," she panted, "I ask you again: Did you say it?" her voice thundered. I was sprawled out on the kitchen floor, my arm shielding my tearing face.

"Ye-ye-yes, I said it," I whimpered.

She bent down toward me with a hand on her hip and with the other she pointed her finger in my face.

"I will not tolerate lying in my house."

As Mrs. Evans advanced toward me, out of reflex I jerked back.

"Do you understand me?" she snarled.

"Ye-ye-yes," I said, trembling.

The ringing telephone interrupted us.

"Hello," she answered sweetly. "Oh, how are you doing? Ha, Ha, Haha," she bellowed out. "Girl, you are a mess! What you say, Ha, ha, ha." She turned toward me. I was sitting in the same position spread out on the floor, arms still shielding my face. She pointed to me and then to the corner. On cue, I scrambled for the corner. She talked on the phone for about an hour, laughing during much of that time. As I stood in the corner for hours, I began to miss my other brothers and sisters. In my heart I cried out for my mother. What had happened to her? Where was my dad? Why was I here?

Later on that day, I heard the door bell ring. I had been sent to my room on the second level of the four-story brownstone. I listened from my bed. I heard feet rushing to the front door. When it opened and I heard, "Hi Mommy, Hi grandma." Mrs. Evans voice replied, "Hi baby, how you doing? Come on in, I'm making these kids some lunch."

"Mommy," the female voice asked, "Where are the kids? Oh there they are; hi boys. Oh Mommy, they are so cute. Is this Eddie?"

Their voices faded because they had moved to another part of the house. I waited. Then I heard footsteps coming up the stairs toward my door. I laid very still and locked my eyes on the bedroom door. The knob turned and the door was pushed open, then in poked a head. It was that of a girl of about thirteen. She entered the room and stared a moment at me. Then she smiled. I smiled back. The girl was pretty chubby, with shoulder length hair. She approached the bed.

"Hi, I'm Stacey," she said.

"Hi, I'm Grace," I replied.

I sat up in the bed and she hugged me. I liked her right away.

"What happened to you?" she asked. "You look like you been in a fight and lost. Look at your hair; it's going every which way. Want me to braid it for you? I'm really good at it."

"All right, Stacey," I replied, climbing off of the bed. "Wait, I don't have a comb or brush."

"Oh, that's okay." She reached inside her pocket book and pulled out a wide-tooth comb. That was convenient because I had thick, nappy hair. When Stacey raked that comb through my hair, I yelped. I liked the finished product, as I looked at those fat corn rows going up and down around my head. I admired my new look. All this I saw through teary eyes. I liked Stacey, and I liked her even more for how she made me look and feel.

"Come downstairs and meet my Mom and Dad," Stacey urged, breaking my concentration.

"No, oh no. I'll get in trouble; I have to stay here."

"Oh, come on," Stacey insisted, pulling me a little by the hand.

"No," I repeated.

"Grandma is nice, you probably made her mad about something and she had to deal with you. I'll be back. I'm going to ask her if you can get up now. Okay?" She hurried toward the door.

"NO!" I cried out," jumping off the bed. I pulled Stacey back and closed the door. "No! I'll get in trouble."

"Move girl, you won't. I'll act like it's all my idea. You know you want to get up." I submitted.

I leaned against the door, listening to Stacey's feet fading downstairs. I waited. Then I heard feet running quickly up the stairs. The feet jumped on the top stairs and raced toward my door. The door flew open as Stacey panted, "Grandma said to get up Gracie, come on." She pulled my arm. "Come on Gracie, Gracie, Gracie."

I was so happy to get out of that prison. I jumped off the bed and ran with my new friend out of the room. We slowed down as we reached the stairs, suppressing giggles. We reached the last step. I grabbed her hand. "Oh Stacey, don't call me Gracie."

Stacey's Mom was very friendly. She looked just like Stacey – very tall, slender, brown-skinned with shoulder length hair. Stacey's Dad was quiet. Stacey had a brother about two years older than she.

Everyone was sitting at the kitchen table. There was a lot of food on the table: hamburgers, franks, and a bottle of Pepsi. Mrs. Evans was throwing some fries into the hot grease. Stacey's Mom called me over. I hurried over to her. Then she pulled out the chair next to her and patted the seat. "Sit down next to me, Grace."

"Oh Stacey, her hair looks so nice. You did a great job baby," she said, turning to her daughter.

"Thank you, Mommy," Stacey replied and gave me a wink.

"She sure did," Mrs. Evans agreed. She approached with a bowl of piping hot french fries.

I froze in my seat ready for the blows to come on me. Instead Mrs. Evans placed the bowl on the table and gave me a hug. "I love you baby. Grandma's sorry she had to beat you, but I love you. I will not stand for lying in this house, all right."

"Yes, Grandma," I said weakly.

"That's my baby," she exclaimed. It made me feel good to hear something like that, but the sentiment didn't last long.

A few days later, she had just come back from the cleaners with her freshly cleaned clothes and pressed suits all covered in plastic. My brothers were playing in the hallway. She greeted us and started down the hall. I had been laying out on the floor playing in her path, so when she passed me, the plastic from the clothes covered my whole face. I began to fight to get it off me. My grandmother looked back at me and kept going. I thought I deserved an apology at least. So I complained.

"Some people just walk on by and don't even say they're sorry!"

My grandmother stopped in her tracks and retraced her steps.

"What did you say?" she asked. "I said you walk on by and don't even say that you are sorry."

My hands were on my hips and I was rolling my eyes. My brothers were startled. Mrs. Evans rushed over and slugged me.

"Don't you ever talk that way to me again; do you hear me?" I was too stunned to answer.

"What? What? You not gonna answer me?" Grandma raised her hand to strike again. I quickly thought of an answer.

"Yes grandma, I'm sorry. I won't do it again."

It was then that I decided not to tolerate any unfair thing from anybody. I was six years old and I felt I could take on anybody. I had stopped longing for my family; they had become a distant memory.

Grandma was a stickler for going to church. Not only was she a saved, Holy Ghost-filled, God-fearing believer, but also a dedicated missionary. She went to church almost seven days a week. Later, we went less often. We weren't what you would call preacher's kids, or maybe we were. I heard preacher's kids are the worst and if that is true, then we were really preacher's kids. My brothers and I sang in the choir although I couldn't sing a lick. I got to lead two songs - "I Said I Wasn't Gonna Tell Nobody" and "Everybody Ought To Know." I was so shy I used to whisper the songs; people could hardly hear me even though I had a microphone.

My best time in church was when we went downstairs to the church basement, where there was Sunday School for the young people. We read Bible verses, sang songs, ate cookies, and drank juice. At certain times we had church down there too, so we could learn about Jesus and practice for upcoming programs like youth day, conventions, and plays.

I had two friends in the church, Sheila and Rhonda, whom I hung out with more than anybody. The two girls would whip anybody who crossed them or their friends. I was glad to be their friend, but I didn't become their friend by butt-kissing; they just liked me and I liked them. I loved getting into mischief with them, and no one was as sneaky or cunning as I. Grandma was strict, so I couldn't afford to be caught.

Chapter 2

Going to School

When I was about six years old, I entered first grade. I was very excited. Grandma took me to school. We stopped in front of a room where lots of kids were reciting something in unison. Then one by one they turned their heads and stared at me. Grandma pulled me into the classroom. My feet felt like lead. I wanted to go home so badly. Finally, we were standing next to the teacher's desk. It was big and had a lot of papers and books on it. Everyone else had little desks.

"Hello, you must be Grace," the teacher greeted with a smile.

I put my finger in my mouth and moved behind Grandma's hips. Her hips could hide anybody and right then were my shield. Grandma yanked me in front of her.

"Say hello to the teacher, Grace." I shook my head in defiance.

"Well, that's okay," the teacher said in her attempt to help. "Grace, you go sit next to Susan."

She pointed to an empty desk in front of her own. Sitting at the desk was Susan, with two long bushy ponytails tied with ribbons, staring blankly at me.

"Okay Grace," Grandma said. "I'm going; I got some errands to run." She turned and walked toward the door. I ran behind her and grabbed her dress tail, screaming.

"I wanna go with you! I don't wanna stay here." My crying must have broken Grandma's heart because her eyes got glassy.

"No baby, stay here. I got to go." The teacher helped her to pry my hands loose. She had me in a tight hold as she encouraged Grandma.

"Go on, go on. She'll be all right."

Grandma waved and left. The teacher continued to talk and soothe me until I was calmer. Many months later I made lots of friends and was more outspoken than all the kids. My teacher said I had the brightest eyes she'd ever seen.

By the time I reached ten years of age, the protective environment of the lower grades no longer existed. In the fifth grade there was a girl named Diana, or "Dee" for short. She was very mouthy, attractive, and popular. Whatever she felt like saying, she said and didn't care whom she hurt. Often I was the object of her candor.

My body had begun to develop. Unfortunately, I was not always prepared hygienically. One day I went to school wearing a white shirt with a rounded collar and dark blue skirt. My grandmother had plaited my hair - one big plait in the front and two big fat ones in the back. I wore bobby socks and penny loafers. I sat across from Diana at a big desk that sat two on each side and one on each end. I was at one of those ends, and Diana sat on my right. Suddenly she blurted out, "Somebody stinks!" Her face crinkled from disgust. Immediately everyone began to smell themselves and say, "Not me." She continued, "Well, I smell it and it's getting on my nerves." Everyone in the class, including the teacher, was smelling themselves. Then someone yelled, "I smell it too. Open the window!"

I was the only one who didn't say anything. I sat very still, because I too had done a self-examination and it was me. My underarms were hot and sweaty and could light up anybody's nose. When Diana noticed me sitting quietly, her eyes narrowed as if she had found the source of the problem. I avoided her gaze. Diana blurted out, "Someone smell Grace." The lynch mob headed my way. Diana smirked at me. Someone grabbed my arm and shrieked profanity. "She stinks, it's Grace." Everybody backed away from me.

Then Diana shouted, "You need a bath!"

I snapped back, "I took one last night."

"Well you needs another one with your funky self." Everyone started laughing.

Embarrassed, I defended, "Your mother needs a bath."

"Ooh," the class mocked.

Diana was ready to go head up and she would have probably whipped me, but I didn't care.

"STOP IT, STOP IT NOW!" the teacher interrupted just in time. "Everyone return to your desks, and Grace, come here honey." Diana and her followers held their noses.

"So what, I don't care," I yelled.

"Grace look at me," the teacher instructed. "Did you take a bath last night?"

"Yes, I did."

"Are you sure?"

"Yes." I don't think she believed me because from the look in her eyes, I knew she had smelled me. But she was polite. "I just didn't have any deodorant, but honest I took a bath," I continued. The teacher gave me an understanding nod and told me to sit down. The mockery had subsided.

*****

During my school years, I was an avid reader and writer. Reading became a hobby. I read horror stories – the bloodier, the better. I read books by

Stephen King, Alfred Hitchcock, John Saul, and Dean Koontz. The occult fascinated me, so I read books on black magic and would try to practice spells at home. I chanted and sat in the dark, burning candles, but nothing happened.

One day my Grandmother found those books and beat the living daylights out of me. "Don't you ever bring these books in my house again," she hollered. "They are of the devil! You hear me?"

"Yes," I cried, but I didn't listen to her. I just made new hiding places.

Simultaneously, I was drawn to the Bible. I would read Daniel, Genesis, and Revelation. I liked stories like David and Goliath and Joseph the Dreamer. I enjoyed reading about Joseph because he was a dreamer like me. I had a recurring dream about my taking a baby by his hind legs and swinging him all around and banging and knocking his head against the wall. There was a room, a crib, and kids around me. The baby had enraged me because he wouldn't stop crying. But after I hurt him he stopped. Suddenly there were screaming voices, police, a white woman. Then it was quiet. I woke up. During the daytime, although I was woke, the images were still in my mind.

I also dreamed about falling and never hitting the bottom. In another recurring dream, monsters and vampires chased me. I was not running fast enough and they are coming at me full speed. There was always an escape for me.

One day I confessed, "Grandma, there are people fighting over me."

"Who are they? Do I know them?" my Grandmother queried.

"I don't think so. I don't know them."

"So how do you know they are fighting over you?"

"I feel them tugging at me even though I can't see them."

She simply dismissed me. I believe she thought I was bonkers, but I felt that someone over my head was always watching me. There were other times I would try to move and my arms, feet, and head and felt like they were cemented to the bed. In my mind I screamed, "Jesus help me, Jesus help me." My pleas sounded like 'blah, blah, blah, blah, blah.' Then I felt something retreat but not without giving me a little shove. A coolness came over my body, and I could move again. I can still feel that war going on over me. I understand it now, but was too young then.

I wasn't too young to understand how to be a trickster. Whenever we went to church there would be a group of kids who went to the store; my brothers and I wanted to go with them. We never had any money, of course, so we would beg church members for a quarter or fifty cents or simply steal it. Being a very crafty, devious girl,

I made up a name of a group that was to help the unfortunate. I told the victims that they had to donate $1.00 and give their names by signing a false document. My victims handed me the $1.00 and signed their names. I made lots of money. I had been friends with Rhonda and Sheila for a long time. We cut out of church together, laughed in church, and talked about boys.

*****

Adam, the boy who lived a few doors down, was my best male friend. To me Adam was a cutie; he had lots of hair he never combed, was taller than I, and had a cool walk. Adam was from Jamaica. I was proud to have him as my friend; he always took time to listen to me. Adam even let me play in his hair and he never made a move on me. My brothers loved him, too.

I had developed physically. I started doing my hair and wearing short dresses. I never considered myself a looker but people, especially other boys, told me I was cute. Once an older man began to pay attention to me and I was afraid. He'd give me money, just to touch me. I never told my grandparents. Adam was the only one with whom I could share it.

I graduated from P.S. 44, Junior High School 258, and was heading toward high school. I broke many boys' hearts along the way. One such instance was with a boy in eighth grade. We were in a program for gifted students known as SAMM, which stood for Science, Art, Math and Music. I was in the science program. I was told that this guy really liked me. So, later, when he asked me if I was going with the school to Great Adventures, I said "Yes." I had stolen the money to go. When the day of the trip came, he asked me to sit next to him. I liked him only as a friend, but I never told him that. All the way there he let me ramble on about nothing and he was very attentive. Once we got to Great Adventures I tried hard to ditch him although he had bought me things. When I even fled from him on foot, he followed me. Once we left the park and got on the bus I told him how I really felt. He was hurt. I also told him I had a sister named Lisa who went to our school and I promised to hook them up because she liked him. Of course I was lying then. He reluctantly agreed.

I didn't treat all guys that way. There were plenty who did treat me nicely, but more who dumped me. There were some to whom I gave money for their birthdays; they took the money and stepped. But all these memories and experiences really did help me in life.

Mrs. Bogan was still a big part of my life. She had gotten permission from foster care to allow my brothers and me to go to sleep away camp. My grandmother took us shopping, packed our bags, gave us a hug, and told us she loved us. I saw tears in her eyes. I also noticed how much she had aged over the years. I had grown to love her very much and I knew she loved me, too.

On the bus each camper wore a tee-shirt bearing the camp's name, YMCA. Some shirts had blue letters, some red, some green, or another color to designate age group and campsite. My brothers sat away from me. I wanted to make my own friends.

Some kids had become couples in those few hours, but they had known each other from previous visits to the camp over the years. It was a long, long bus ride; but we finally reached our destination, hot, tired, but very happy. Once we settled in we sat around camp fires, sang songs, roasted marshmallows, went on treasure hunts, swam, canoed, played warrior games where we had to conquer flags, and ran relay races. The YMCA was the best camp I remember ever attending.

Chapter 3

High School

After I graduated from junior high school, I was enrolled in William H. Maxwell School in East New York. I had wanted to go to that high school because I wanted a career in cosmetology. I later changed my career to nursing.

My grandparents were aging by then and Mrs. Bogan was in the process of moving my brothers and me to a younger couple. In the following two and a half years I changed more homes than people do their clothes.

I accepted Jesus Christ into my life at age twelve, and entered high school happy and energetic. I was very excited because I had big dreams of all the things I wanted to become and do in life.

Maxwell wasn't as I expected. There were always people fighting, lots of "butches and femmes," and people trying to out dress one another. This was the era of Run-DMC, Kool Moe

47

Dee, and LL Cool J. I heard The Fat boys went to Boys and Girls High School down the street from me. Kids wore Levi jeans, Lee jeans, Cazals (eye glasses), Adidas, Pumas with wide laces, wind breakers, Kangos, big dukey chains (name plates of gold and silver), and four finger rings. They were either Black or Latino. These students used to break dance and pop while carrying giant radios around.

When I first went to my cosmetology class, I was a very quiet student who didn't give anyone any problems. In the class there was a girl named Ingrid Stephens who was called 'Peaches' by her close friends. She had a very big mouth and was a comedian. The teacher didn't like her very much. Peaches was very disrespectful to her and never heeded anything the teacher told her. When we were told to apply one coat of polish, Peaches applied two, or more. Somehow no matter how neat we painted each other's nails the teacher always knew when we didn't listen.

During this period we were moved from Grandma's house to the Keith's house. I only remember their last name, mostly because I had a brother named Keith. There were lots of tears shed when we left Grandma's, but I thought that I could be finally free to do as I wanted: dress more in style, and go where I pleased.

The Keith's bought us new clothes, shoes, and the wife pressed my hair. We would often take trips to my favorite place, the Public Library. One day while we were headed home (we had decided to walk that day) we were about to cross the street when I felt someone looking at me. I looked around to find a young man just sitting there staring. I stared back, hoping he would drop his eyes but that made him stare harder. I turned around and proceeded across the street with my brothers and the Keith's. Once I was across the street, I glanced back just to find he had turned all the way around, still staring. About a half block up he was still staring. Even when he became a dot in my sight, he was still staring.

The Keith's were Muslims, their beliefs went against all my Christian beliefs. Sometimes they would try to introduce their beliefs to me, but I was a very good debater.   They didn't eat pork, but drank lots of Pepsi. They had two girls and one boy: Cynthia, Nicole, and Michael. Cynthia sucked her finger, as did I. She was very clingy to me. My brother Anthony and Cynthia were pretty close only because they both were very silly. When he teased her, she would snap right back. That made matters worse because he teased her all the more. Nicole was the family snitch, and Michael was the spoiled cry baby.

We always went to Green Acres to go shopping for clothes. Mrs. Keith bought me pants, shirts and other clothes. They were better than the clothes Grandma gave me to wear.

By then Peaches and I had become good friends. She introduced me to her group of friends: Michelle, Porche, Darlene, and Rhonda whom I knew already because we went to church together. Peaches always teased me and called me churchy or goody-goody. Whenever we met in the bathroom between classes she said, "Grace, wait outside, or don't smoke around Grace; she's a good girl." Porche was also a Christian who always wore skirts. I believe she and Michelle were Spanish. Porche was very pretty, with long hair and had all the latest styles (even though she wore skirts all the time). Michelle was also pretty, but more tom-boyish and tough. She and Peaches could whip anybody even though they both were short. Michelle was going out with a much older man, whom I thought was her father. Darlene Henderson was another tough one that no one messed with. I hung with this group of pretty girls no one dared mess with.

One day a girl sitting next to me in class was putting on make-up and she caught me watching her. She asked me if I wanted to try some. I did. Secretly, this was a big deal for me. I wanted it to look on me as it did on her. So she put the make-up on me and when she finished, she liked it. I looked in the mirror and smiled. Peaches, everybody in the group, and several other class mates agreed. So when I went home I got Mrs. Keith's permission to wear make-up.

Another day in school, a friend was applying my make-up. Another girl blurted out that my friend didn't need any make up but I sure did. Everyone laughed. I laughed too out of nervousness, because I was scared of this girl. I started having flashbacks of Diana and how she used to tease me. I was sitting with Darlene and Rhonda when this bully sent a message that she was going to kick my "ugly so and so" and she wanted to see me in the back of the classroom. I didn't move because I knew the type of school I went to, and I saw girls attacked all the time. I didn't want to be one of them. So I didn't move. The girl repeated the message word for word. Darlene got mad and slammed her fist on the table. "You tell that b---- that Darlene Henderson said if she wants to step to my girl, she gots to go through me first." The girl scurried away but she didn't have to deliver the message because the bully heard it loudly and clearly. She never gave me any more problems.

At home things began to get uneasy. I was getting older and more set in my ways. I didn't go to church so I began to wander away from my Christian beliefs and became more rebellious.

I was becoming friends with my neighbor's daughter, Ericka. She was from South Carolina. Once I had been the one the guys in the neighborhood pursued. Ericka became the new object of their pursuits. She would sit on her stairs and I would sit on mine, but we never said anything to each other.

As guys passed by, they would start to say something to me, but see her, and whistle or honk at her instead. I felt a little jealous at first but I began to soften toward her because she seemed very lonely. She was an only child and was up here for the summer. One day she spoke to me and we clicked right away. Later we became inseparable. I would go to her house but she never came to mine. The Keith's didn't really like her. She was very fast, outspoken, and said whatever she felt. Soon all the neighborhood kids began to hang out on her stairs. Of course, Mrs. Keith had a few things to say about it. She and I stood toe to toe, but nothing kept me away from Ericka, Peaches, or any of my friends.

One day Cynthia and I went to Prospect Park to jump rope and hang out. Some girls wanted to fight Cynthia, but she was my little sister and I wasn't having it. Once we got home I began to re-enact the scene before Ericka, my brothers and some other kids from the neighborhood. Meanwhile Mrs. Keith was standing by the window listening. Suddenly her head appeared outside her window and she yelled for Cynthia and me to get upstairs. The other kids teased, "Oh, Oh, you in trouble." I rebelled inwardly. Once inside Mrs. Keith asked me to tell her what happened and I refused. She then turned to Cynthia and asked her what happened, but she refused, too. "All right then," Mrs. Keith retired. Then she headed toward her bedroom and returned with a thick leather belt. Cynthia was scared. "All right Mommy, I'll tell you. I'll tell you!" I stood still and refused. She gave Cynthia a few whacks and sent her howling to bed. When Mrs. Keith hit me, I refused to budge. She hit me again and shoved me a little, knocking me off balance. I retraced my steps and folded my arms across my chest.

"You will do as I say," she commanded.

"No I won't," I yelled.

"I will not have rebellious kids in my house," Mrs. Keith insisted.

"I don't want to stay in your stinking house," I retorted. That did it! She called Mrs. Bogan and told her what happened. Mrs. Bogan was furious because I had been hit, so she moved my brothers and me. Cynthia was hysterical, so was her sister and brother. I hugged Ericka, told her I'd stay in touch, and my brothers and I got into Mrs. Bogan's car. It would be many years before I saw them again.

"Out With the Old, In With the New"

We were moved to the MacCalesters. They were Christians. The father was the pastor of a church. I still attended Maxwell High School and discovered that I'd moved close to Peaches' home.

Peaches had suggested that we go to school together and hang out together, too. I wasn't so sure, for my new guardians looked strict and were really into church.

The MacCalesters went to church every Sunday and during the week. They had five children, one of whom was a boy around my age. I didn't like it there at all. We couldn't go outside the gate and play or mingle with neighborhood kids, so we just sat on the front steps all the time. My brother Anthony was their favorite. Mrs. C. eventually let him out to play football while the rest of us sat on the steps.

One of the children was a foster child named Maxine, whom they had since birth. She was left in the hospital by her natural Mom. This was the only home she ever knew. Maxine clung to me as her little sister clung to her. She wanted to do her hair like me, walk like me and talk like me. She wanted to be my clone. She was very nosey and talked too much. My brothers despised her. When grown-ups talked, she appeared miraculously between them, looking from one to the other.

When my brothers and I were talking, she appeared out of the blue and jumped right in our conversation.

I shared a bedroom with Maxine and her sister. Those two would be up for hours laughing and playing. I would nudge Maxine in the ribs because she insisted on laying next to me. I didn't want to lay next to either of them, but there was only one bed.

I was getting into rap music and started writing rhymes. I went by the name Lady MC. I would be downstairs listening to rap and be inspired to write. Peaches and the crew liked my music. My attitude was changing. I became very moody and fed up with people around me. I wanted to go to school and fit in. I wanted a name plate, name earrings, and new clothes. I was hungry half the time because we didn't get much to eat, and the shoes I had were run over or had holes in them. I hardly got any allowance because anytime I voiced my opinion or talked back, Mrs. C took it away. When her son, who didn't speak to anyone, spoke to me, it was an honor. I wanted to be his friend because he was really cool.

We went to church every Sunday; I sang in the choir. I repented and turned to Jesus once again. Every time people got on the prayer line and hands were laid on them, they fell back. I noticed when they laid hands on Maxine and she fell back, they made her get up. They told her to stop faking. That made me believe that everyone was faking.

One day I was sitting in church next to Stacey and there was an altar call. As hands were laid on people they shook and praised God. I said within myself that they were faking. All of a sudden *my* body started to shake a little, just a little. Then slowly it increased. My hands shook until it became noticeable to Stacey. She leaned over and whispered, "Are you all right?" I immediately sat on my hands, but then my feet shook uncontrollably. I was scared! Then an usher came down the aisle, grabbed my hand, and pulled me out of my row into the aisle. I was crying by then. I didn't understand what was going on and why my body was shaking so. "Say 'thank you Jesus'" she kept saying. I obeyed. I almost collapsed, but she caught me and held me in her arms. She said, "Don't be afraid, it's the anointing of the Holy Spirit."

"Huh?" I said to myself. I didn't understand what she was talking about.

*****

There was a lady who lived across the street from me during that time. She took care of the handicapped and people with mental disabilities. She would let me come over and look through bags of clothes to see what fit me so I could have something decent to wear to school, but a lot of her stuff was outdated or just too big. I would thank her anyway.

The C's were out one day and asked her to baby-sit my brothers, Maxine, and me. I was about fifteen years old and felt I didn't need a baby-sitter, but across the street we went. I was in the bathroom playing with my hair and putting on a little make-up when I heard the front door open. Her son came in. He was slow. He came in the house babbling about something, and as I emerged from the bathroom, he fastened his eyes on me. I ignored him.

His sister had a drooling problem, so when she approached me I became very uneasy. She leaned forward and put her face close to mine. I could feel her breath on my face. Still I ignored her but prayed that none of her drool touched me. It was too late, for two or three drops got on my arm. When I screamed, the startled lady shooed her daughter away. I pointed to my arm in dis-gust, and she saw the spit. She told me to go to the bathroom and wash my arm. Her daughter babbled slowly, "I'm sorry, I'm sorry." Her mom apologized but I continued screaming. I washed my arm vigorously, praying that I didn't have a disease or anything contagious. When I finally came out, I slowly headed toward the living room, hoping no one would notice me. I found a chair and sat far into the corner so there would be no room for either of them to sit or stand next to me. Still they chose to stand and stare. I was glad when the C's son came to take us back to the house. Once we got inside, Mrs. C's son asked me to come with him because he had to ask me something. I followed because I knew he was in love with a young lady who didn't like him the same way. I often heard him tear up his room in rage because she refused to go out with him. That was her loss. I finally went to my room to find him just standing there.

"What is it?" I asked.

"Could you close the door? I want to ask you something," he said.

I closed the door. I felt I had finally touched base with this really cool guy, and he was about to share some of his secrets. I saw nothing wrong in having a male for a best friend because Adam was my friend and there was no intimacy at all. He told me about the girl, about sports, and his future. I didn't add or take away from the conversation; I just gave an attentive ear. We eventually got up and left the room because his parents were home and I didn't want them to get the wrong idea.

*****

That night Maxine and her sister were goofing off as usual and I nudged Maxine and told them to quit it, or else. I dozed off and was suddenly awakened. The bed was moving just so slightly and I heard whispering. It was Maxine and her sister. The bed was shaking a little, then it stopped. There was more whispering and shaking. My heart beat so fast that I wondered if I added to the shaking. What on earth were they whispering about? I lay very still and strained to hear. "You are J.R. and I am Sue Ellen."

"No!" That was Maxine's voice and she said it harshly. "You are Sue Ellen and I'm J.R." I could hear her sister whining because she didn't get her way. Maxine told her to hush. I could tell by her voice she was very irritated by her sister's whining. I gave a fake cough, grunted and turned over, and started to do my fake snoring. The shaking had stopped abruptly. I laid still, and continued my fake snoring. Then the shaking resumed but not hard just slowly. I peeked through my eyelids and saw something moving up and down, up and down. I opened my eyes a little more, then all the way. I saw a covered hump moving up and down. I reached out ever so slowly and grabbed hold of that blanket and yanked it back. Underneath was Maxine on top of her little sister; she was about to bring her bottom down to meet her sister's already raised bottom. Startled, they both yelped and cried. They ended up blaming each other. "Hush," I told them.

"Are you gonna tell on us?" Maxine and her sister asked at the same time.

"I don't know. Go to sleep or I'll tell right now!"

Then Maxine scrambled off her sister and laid with her back to me. Her sister turned her back to Maxine and laid there. I turned my back on them. I went to sleep with a smile on my face. Having dirt on a person sure felt powerful.

*****

I was eventually moved out of that room into a room upstairs with my brother and Mrs. C's brother, who was hardly there. I would sit in my room writing out raps and recording them on my tape deck. I would wash my hair, press it, then sit outside. One particular day my brothers and Maxine accompanied me on the steps then eventually her sister and little brother joined us. It was a hot day. Anthony was outside playing football as usual and our baby-sitter's son had come out and was standing in his yard. My brother Keith was a great imitator, so he chose to mock her son. I was laughing so hard that I fell over holding my side. Maxine made it worse because she was pointing and looking at the lady's son. Of course he figured out we were laughing at him. He

pointed at us and told us to stop teasing him.
Keith pointed back, mocking his every word.
Anthony looked over at us and said "Y'all better
leave him alone." The lady's son was getting angry
and started kicking his garbage cans and then his
gate, but Keith kept the jokes coming. All of a
sudden the man hopped over the fence with one
hand and ran toward us. Rage was written all over
his face. We scrambled off the steps. The guys in
the street went in opposite directions. Keith ran
inside first, then Maxine's sister and brother.
Maxine and I were last in tow. As Maxine and I
reached the iron door, my brother, or one of the
others, locked Maxine and me out. By then the
man had leaped our fence and had started to
pounce on us. Maxine's fingers were holding on
to the bars in the window. We both were screaming, enough to wake the dead. When he swung,
I grabbed Maxine and used her as a shield. She
caught most of the blows and I caught one on my
head. I swung back and delivered some to his
body. This only angered him more as Maxine's
body caught his fury. We screamed. Eventually
Mr. C and the man's Mom came outside. Mr. C
got between Maxine and me and commanded the
man back across the street. The mother called her
son, who immediately went back into his yard.
When Mr. C. heard of our teasing, he took off his
belt to lay it on us but Maxine tried to blame

Keith. I twisted her story so that she got it for all of us. No one could ever outsmart me.

Being fifteen wasn't easy for me. I was becoming more depressed and moody because I wasn't dressing like the other kids. My shoes had holes in them and I didn't go to the laundry. I still had to deal with bullies at school. Peaches and I were still cool and I was close with the other girls but they weren't with me all the time.

Meanwhile, Mrs. C's son, Jay, and I were steering toward a more sexual relationship, stopping short of actual intercourse. He was more into, bumping, touching, and feeling. Toward the daytime, he would act as if he never knew me and whatever happened the night before never happened at all.

It reminded me of my younger days when men and women had the same lust over me. Was I cursed? I didn't know. What I did know was I hated my life and wished I were never born. If life were a deck of cards and being here for other people's sexual pleasures was my hand, I been dealt a bad hand!

I told my social worker all about it. I didn't hold anything back. I told her about my younger days when I had to deal with people humping, feeling, groping me and how the problems continued as I got older. I told her about not having money for clothes, shoes, and personal hygiene. Mrs. Bogan was my only grown-up best friend and guardian, and I knew she would defend me just as she had so many times in the past. She said she would get me out of the mess as soon as she could. She also told me I was getting older and set in my ways. That was the thing that stopped people from fostering or adopting teenagers. However, she promised to help. In my heart I knew she would as always.

*****

One day a bully in my nursing class confronted me. I was sitting in the second row of the classroom, and her desk was in the front row to my right. She was running her mouth, telling other girls about some unfortunate girl whom she beat up just for crossing her path. As she was giving her version of her encounter, I looked over at the teacher, who had stopped teaching and was listening, too. All of a sudden, I spotted a movement on my desk. It was a roach scurrying across my desk. My heart almost stopped! I pretended it wasn't there, but the bully had already spotted it, too. She shouted, "Look! That so-and-so has a roach on her desk! Look everybody she got a roach on her desk!" My pressure must have risen. I was filled with rage. My teeth bit down on my bottom lip, a habit I developed when I was furious. The girl kept on cursing at me. Everybody was laughing and pointing at me and the roach as if we had become one.

"She's got roaches in her crib y'all!"

I yelled back. "I ain't got no roaches in my crib!"

"You do so. Everyone got roaches in their cribs!"

I snapped back, "If that's the case what you worried about it for?"

"Because at least we keep them home; we don't bring them to school," she mocked. The class roared with laughter.

"Well, how do you know it's my roach and not yours?"

"Oooo!" the others instigated.

"What? What did you say b----?"

"You heard me. He looks like you but bears a stronger resemblance to your mother!"

By then everyone was laughing at her, not at me.

"Oh snap! she dissed you," one yelled across the room.

"Yup! You going to put up with that?" someone else taunted.

I pressed on. "You're ugly! With a face like a bulldog! Where's your leash? Woof! Woof!"

Then she warned, "Watch, you and I have lunch together. I'm going to kick your so-and-so; watch and see."

The class was in an uproar. I didn't care because I was very angry and bitter; maybe fighting would give me some relief from all I felt inside. I was going to fight with all I had. If all I had wasn't good enough, at least I would leave this world trying.

News traveled fast in Maxwell High School, so Peaches and my girls found out about the fight. Everyone who could either cut class or get a bathroom pass to meet in the lunchroom was there. They came to see the fight of the century. It was a great turn-out. If I had known better, I would have charged everyone by the seat. Peaches and the girls cut class, too. They found me on the lunchroom line. Encircling me, they walked up to where the lunch lady gave me my lunch. I collected my milk and headed toward a table. Peaches and the gang were still walking with me. Bodies parted quietly as we moved along the room. Everyone was quietly watching, not wanting to miss anything. I walked right by the bully's table. She didn't say one word. In fact, when we looked over at her she looked down as if concentrating on her lunch. There was to be no fight, so many students continued chattering, others returned to their classrooms, and those who cut class that period hung out in the lunchroom. I sat next to my friends Karen and Peaches before they returned to class.

"That was close, Grace," Karen said.

"I know, but I don't care."

"Good thing you're friends with Peaches and her crew, otherwise I would be visiting your grave."

"Yeah. But still I would have peace any ways," I responded.

"What did I miss?" Angel asked.

Angel wasn't what you would call an outcast. She was the same height as I, very pretty, and shy around people she didn't know. She always wore tight pants, jean jackets with the collar turned up, and her hair long. The guys whistled when she walked, but she didn't like it. If she was eating with us and a piece of meat fell out of her sandwich or food was lodged against her mouth, she'd throw everything away. Angel always felt someone was watching her. On the other hand, if that happened to me, there was no way that I'd get rid of my lunch. I stayed hungry because we didn't get much to eat at home. So if the meat fell, I picked it up and ate it. I didn't care who watched.

Karen, by then, had gotten up to go to the bathroom, this would be her third time. When she returned I said, "Karen I've been watching you for some weeks now, what's up? Why do you go to the bathroom so much?"

"I don't know and I'm always thirsty, too."

"I know, I see you always ask for my juice and you already drank several juices of your own. Just stop drinking so much and you won't have to go to the bathroom so much," I said.

"Yeah right, I can't help it," she replied. I was worried about her. It wasn't her weight, for she was always thin. I just had a feeling I couldn't shake.

The bell rang. I had one more class. It was Friday, Spring was here, and we all were anxious to get out of school. I told Karen and Angel I would see them the following Monday. We all got up and rushed to class. I didn't see Karen on Monday, because over the weekend she went into a diabetic coma and a few days later she died. It wasn't her death that upset me but the fact that she was so nice. She didn't deserve it. It was I who should have died. I hated my life and wanted out.

As Spring turned into Summer, I started hanging with different girls. In each of my classes I had a friend with whom I would hang out. My baby-sitter across the street had started getting more decent clothes, so I was wearing lots of jeans and tighter shirts. I began to imitate Angel's hairstyles, and she gave me advice about make-up and clothes. I was a good listener and student. Lots of guys tried to talk to me but I played hard to get.

Peaches was still a big part of my life. She always took time to listen. She knew I was having problems at home and tried her best to make school as fun and interesting as possible. When school closed for the summer vacation, my brothers and I did nothing. Anthony played football or simply laid around. The rest of us sat around on the stoop and watched people and cars go by. Inside I was contemplating my years. I was getting more tense when the summer ended, for September was upon me and that meant I needed a new wardrobe. I couldn't wait to see Peaches and the rest of the crew.

September was chaotic. The ladies in the office had our schedules mixed up, lockers screwed up, and some of us who took buses and trains to school had to wait a few days to get our passes for the year. That confusion sent other students on a stealing spree.

Mrs. Bogan must have had a talk with my foster parents because they gave me one hundred dollars. This to me was gold. They took me to a store in Green Acres. I bought personal items, toiletries, some blouses, a skirt, a pair of Lees, a pair of shoes, a dress, and hat for church. I washed my hair, pressed and curled it, took a shower and went to bed with the biggest smile on my face. Some time later I raised my head and looked around the semi-dark room. I saw my dresser on which lay my toothpaste, toothbrush, deodorant, and make-up; and on the chair were my clothes, a white blouse with a pair of light blue Lee pants.

Under the chair were my new black shoes. I smiled. I couldn't wait to go to school.

When I awakened, I beat my brothers to the bathroom. I washed my face, put some lotion on my skin, dressed, combed my hair, and exited my room. I greeted my brothers, who ignored me. I borrowed Anthony's wind breaker. I loved his jacket because it bore the "Westinghouse" logo. George Westinghouse was a high school for guys only and since I went to an all girls' school, that jacket made me popular with the ladies and cool with the guys. Maxine spotted me first.   "Oh! Grace you look so nice and pretty, too!" She touched my arm and followed me down the hall like a lap dog. I shoved her arm off me because I didn't want her messing up my jacket. I heard the door bell ring. I didn't bother to see who it was.

"Grace, it's for you," Maxine yelled.

I rushed to the front door and tripped over something someone left in the hallway.

"Who is it?" I asked Maxine, who was just standing at the door with a grin on her face.

"I don't know. They wouldn't tell me," she said.

"They? Who's they?" I wondered.

I shoved her out of the way; she barely budged. There standing at my front door were Peaches and Michelle. When they saw me, their faces lit up.

"Grace! Look at you, you look so-o nice," Peaches exclaimed.

"Yeah, you do Grace," Michelle agreed.

Peaches insisted that I turn around.

"Look at that shape; Grace you have a nice shape, you should wear pants more often, girl!" Peaches hugged me. "Now, get your books and coat; we're going to school together. We came to pick you up."

I was shocked. They never went to school with me, except when we took the J train home together. I got my books and jacket. "Bye everyone," I yelled. No one answered me, but I didn't care. I ran out the door.

"Grace, Michelle and I were talking," Peaches piped up. I should have known that there was discussion about me. "We were saying how cute you would look with your ears pierced instead of wearing those clip-ons," she continued. *Ears pierced! They want to pierce my ears or drill a hole in them is more like it.*

"Now you don't have to if you don't want to Grace. Okay?" Peaches reassured.

"It's all right, you can," I answered nonchalantly.

"Great!" Peaches squealed. "Now after school we'll go to Michelle's house and pierce your ears; it's gonna be so fun!"

"It sounds like you had this planned," I said.

"Oh no! No! No!" Peaches and Michelle said together. "We just thought of it, really."

"Oh, okay," I resigned. *And fish can fly.*

From home all the way to school, I received a lot of attention from guys on the street. Peaches was there telling them to back off. I liked the attention.

That day marked one of the happiest days of my life. It was the day I got to wear new clothes and shoes. I felt like a new woman.

After school, I went to Michelle's house. I was very nervous about letting them pierce my ears, but they insisted they knew what they were doing. After settling ourselves in the apartment, Peaches started shouting out commands.

"Grace, sit down here in this chair," she ordered, pointing to a kitchen chair.

"Michelle, get some ice! I'll get the needle and thread." Peaches couldn't find any white thread but chose brown thread instead.

"Peaches, I don't have no ice," Michelle said.

"Well, you got any frozen meat or something?" she asked.

"Yeah."

"We will use that then."

The girls put the frozen food against my ear lobes. It was so cold. After a while Peaches asked if I could feel her pinching my ears. I couldn't.

"Come on Michelle, quick, let's stick the needle in," Peaches said.

Michelle was working on the other ear. Peaches warned me not to move. I didn't feel the needles go in, but halfway through, my ears started thawing. The needles were stuck. It started to hurt. Peaches and Michelle tried to freeze my ear lobes again but it was useless. Peaches told me to brace myself and they both rammed the needles in my ear lobes. I felt a pinch and yelped. Peaches announced proudly that the needles went through successively. My ears were sore a few days but I was happy. I had pierced ears!

*****

Later that week Mrs. Bogan called to tell me she had good news. She had found a new home for me and I would be leaving in a few months. The new family lived in Long Island, and I was the only one of my siblings who was leaving. I was devastated but excited. My brothers and I had always been together. Soon we were going to be split up.

As the months went by, things stayed tense at the C's. I went to church but I had lost my zeal. All I wanted was my freedom. I stayed in my room mostly and had gotten into rap music very heavily. I was into LL Cool J, Run-DMC, and Curtis Blow. I bought a name belt that read "Lady MC" and people started questioning me. I got mixed reviews once people heard me. I didn't care.

* * * * *

One day my nursing teacher asked me to stay after class. After everyone cleared out she revealed that she had an application for me to work at a camp for the handicapped. It was called UCP of America (United Cerebral Palsy). She thought it would be really nice for me, especially since I was going through some problems at home. I was a great student, who would make a great nurse someday. I took the application and thanked her, grateful for a chance to make money. Besides, I was sixteen years old and a change in my life would have been refreshing.

I told Mrs. Bogan what my teacher said and that it was a summer job. Mrs. Bogan was thrilled. It was the perfect job for me. I went to school on Monday and told Peaches; she was ambivalent.

I went to the job interview and received the job. I was told how much I would be receiving for the summer. Mrs. Bogan saw to it that I received an allowance to go shopping for all my needs.

Those last two weeks at the C's were like being in a whirlwind. I believe they were glad to see me go. My brothers weren't. Keith had begun to shut himself off from everyone and everything. He had threatened to kill himself if we couldn't stay together; Eddie wouldn't talk to anyone and Anthony got wrapped up with friends in the neighborhood. It broke my heart to leave them, but I couldn't be their mom anymore. There were battles they would have to fight on their own. Our lives had turned into four different roads.

"A Taste of Freedom"
1985

I said good-bye to my brothers, Maxine, the C's, and my neighbors. They were crying but I wasn't. I had always wanted to be free, and here was my opportunity. But my heart pained for my brothers. I was hoping and praying they would be fine. I walked away and didn't look back; if I had, I would never have left.

I got to Manhattan very early. I remember dragging a large suitcase on the bus. I had bought new clothes, shoes and sneakers. I refused to take any of those funky, dirty clothes with me. I loathed the hand-me-downs. The outfit I wore to Manhattan was new.

I had to meet camp counselors, camp directors and other employers at the huge UCP building. The bus was already there. I approached one of the buses because I saw a line of teenagers waiting.

"Excuse me," I said to a girl at the end of the line.

"Yeah, Uh-huh," she said and turned around. She was blonde, slim, very pretty. She was wearing a tee-shirt, slacks and sneakers. I studied her face for a moment and she smiled at me. She seemed friendly enough, so I smiled back.

"Hi," she said.

"Oh hi. Um - could you tell me if y'all are just standing here to load your bags, or do you have to go somewhere to check in first?"

"Yes and yes," she said. "Yes, this is where we load our bags, and yes, you have to go somewhere to sign in first."

She was smiling a toothy grin and staring directly into my eyes. She made me uncomfortable, but I didn't want her to know that. So I stared back, grinning too.

"Where do I sign in?"

She pointed toward two glass doors of the building and said, "Go through there, down the hall, make a left, then a right, go straight down that hallway and there's a door marked 'Shirley Hinds.' Knock, and that's where you sign in."

Her eyes were the bluest I'd ever seen. I hadn't seen many white people before, just my teachers, a few Spanish kids who looked white, but not many my age who were actually white. She'd given me so many directions that I hoped I remembered them all. I thanked her, gathered up my suitcase, and headed toward the glass doors.

"Hey," she called out. There was a lot of talking going on and noisy, polluted cars passing by.

"What's your name?" she asked. I rolled my suitcase back over and shoved my hand into her outstretched hand. She had a firm grip, which threw me off a little.

"Grace," I told her. "Grace Johnson, what's yours?"

"Brenda, Brenda McQueen."

I thought she would say something like Sally or Jane, but Brenda was a cool name.

"Nice to meet you Brenda. All right see ya," I said.

"See ya too," she replied.

I retraced my steps toward those glass doors. Once I got inside I looked around a moment. The place was huge! It had the highest ceiling I ever saw. There were all sorts of glass front stores, boutiques, and shiny floors that went for miles. I kept hearing 'ding, ding'. It was coming from the elevator. People in suits and carrying brief cases were getting on and off. Well-dressed women were talking or rushing toward the elevator doors. I got out of my trance and headed toward the hallway on my left; it was the only hallway there. I followed Brenda's directions and found Shirley Hind's office. After I knocked a voice called me in. There was Shirley; I remembered her from my interview.

"Hello," she greeted me with a smile. "Grace, right?" She'd remembered my name.

"Yes, I'm Grace."

"Sit down Grace, I'm going to sign you in and give you a badge with your name on it. There is still a little paperwork you have to fill out. Also, you were supposed to give us at least two phone numbers in case of emergency, but you left that part blank."

She said that someone named Mrs. Bogan called her office and she told her she was my social worker. Mrs. Bogan told Shirley to keep in touch with her and left her phone number. I didn't intend to give her the C's phone number.

I filled out paperwork, signed in, and left Shirley's office wearing my badge. It was white, and read "C-O-U-N-S-E-L-O-R" in blue letters, and had my name underneath. If I lost it I'd have to pay five dollars for a new one. I wore that badge with pride. I rejoined the other teenagers who were boarding the bus; the long line had narrowed down to about seven or eight people. When I finally got up to a man with a clip board, he jerked his head up and looked at me. He found my name with ease and put a check by it. I noticed there were several names that weren't checked off. I guess they were either on their way or not coming.

"Is that the only bag you got?" he asked pointing at my suitcase.

"Yes."

"Okay, great. You are one of the easiest persons to work with so far. You just wouldn't believe it man, what a day!"

I smiled and didn't say anything. He quickly grabbed my bag like it weighed nothing at all and shoved it in the luggage department on the outside of the bus. It was loaded with so many, many bags.

"I hope you got your name on your bag," he added. I did. "Well, you can get on the bus. I see you signed in already 'cause you got your badge. Sit anywhere you like; the bus isn't quite full yet. Okay hon?" He held out his hand, which I shook. He wished me good luck.

The bus was cool and spacious. I headed toward the back; I didn't like front rows. There wasn't anyone back there. I had glanced at people as I moved down the aisle but I didn't see Brenda. Maybe she was on another bus. I settled down in a seat across from the bathroom. My hands folded in my lap, I looked out the window. I was sixteen years old and on my own, just for a little while. This was my first job. I had been through so much through the years, yet time seemed to go by so fast. I took a deep breath and exhaled very slowly.

After we waited about forty-five minutes, the bus never did get any fuller. Two buses in front of mine were already packed. It was time to depart.

I said good-bye to all five boroughs and hello to life in the country setting. We went toward up-state New York. I loved the scenery and long ride. It didn't matter if I didn't have a seating partner; I cherished the peace and quiet. It gave me time to appreciate nature.

We entered the campsite about six hours later. We were all tired. Shirley was there already; she had driven ahead of us, along with other camp directors and counselors. Shirley began to speak through a horn. "Attention everyone, please stop talking a moment and let me speak."

I took that moment to glance at a few people. Everyone seemed to know one another either from the bus or from before. I glanced around for Brenda but she was nowhere in sight.

"Now! I have a list here along with Dave, Rod, and Sheila. These are counselors who will be helping me and you also. If you have any questions please ask me or one of them," Shirley continued. She pointed to each of them and said their names. She pointed to an older woman standing in the rear of them with her arms folded across her chest. "This is Mrs. Quinn, and she is the nurse. Any problems, please see her." Mrs. Quinn unfolded her arms and gave a little wave. Shirley pointed to the house behind her. "This is Mrs. Quinn's office, the time, days and what have you are all on the sign outside her door. Are there any questions?"

"Yeah," someone shouted. My eyes traveled to find the speaker's voice. They fell on a tall, brown-skinned guy.

"Where are we gonna sleep at?"

Immediately several hands went up and some talked out of turn. "When is lunch?" "Where are the campers?" "When are they getting here?" "Can we use the pool?" Questions were shouted from all directions.

"Calm down everyone. I'll answer your questions one at a time," Shirley responded. Her face was becoming strained. "Now behind you, you see several cabins spaced out all over the area; Rod will be giving everyone their assigned cabin. The pool is available to you. Steve and his lifeguards, who you will be meeting tomorrow, are in charge of that."

Shirley dismissed us. We all swarmed Rod and his team. I was assigned to cabin two. I headed across the field.

"Hey Grace, wait up!" I turned around to see who was calling me. It was Brenda jogging toward me, dragging a heavy looking bag. She was with three other girls. We hugged. "Grace, this is Jessica, Patricia and Crystal."

"Hi," we quickly greeted one another.

"You look familiar," Jessica said. I never saw someone who had such pretty black skin, I thought.

"Where you from?" she asked. I told her Brooklyn. She was from there, too.

"What part?" she pressed.

"Bed-Stuy do or die, and Bushwickville never ran never will," I replied.

"Yeah, I'm from do or die. I've seen you before," she said.

"Did you go to P.S. 44?" I asked.

"Nope."

"What about Junior High School 258?"

"Nope."

"Maxwell?"

"Naw, I went to Boys and Girls High School."

"I don't know, I must got one of those faces," I joked.

"What cabin are you in Grace?" Brenda asked.

"I'm in cabin two; what about you?" I replied.

"I'm in cabin six. We all four are. But I'll check you out, okay? See you later, nice meeting you too, Grace."

My cabin was directly across the field. There were five cots there and rows of cubicles. Four cots were occupied already. I entered and didn't say a word at first. When other girls greeted me, I returned the courtesy. I took the cot by the door and sat down. My roommates were very talkative. We introduced ourselves to one another. Harriet's cot was next to mine. She was a lot older than we, maybe in her late twenties. Yolanda slept in the middle cot and Cecile at the end. Across from us, to my left, was Roberta's cot and to my right was Shaquisha's. Everyone was very friendly and chatty, except Shaquisha and me.

After two weeks, the campers came in by the bus-loads. I was given a print out with my camper's description, symptoms, hobbies, bad habits, likes and dislikes, age, color, etc. I was so scared that day I saw the campers get off the bus. Some were in wheelchairs, some weighing 200 pounds or more, others were very thin, blind, and/or disfigured. My camper was on the last bus.

A camper got off the bus wearing a white tee shirt, shorts and baseball cap. He was short, about the height of a six-year old. He looked frightened. There were three other campers left on the bus. One was in a wheel chair; her body was totally deformed. My heart slowed. The "six-year old" was standing on the side of the bus. I headed toward him. He stopped fidgeting and looked at me; then he broke into the biggest smile. A few teeth were missing, but he was cute. "What's your name?" I asked him. He shrugged his shoulders and kept smiling at me.

"You don't know your name?" I asked, stooping next to him. "Come on, tell me your name." He just shrugged and kept grinning at me. I noticed a tag on his shirt; it read "Paul Wilson." He was mine. I grabbed his hand, collected his bags, and headed for his cabin.

I had been Paul's counselor for two weeks. He wasn't a bad camper but he was known to wander, have fits and bite. He never did those things with me. There were a lot of rules to follow. I messed up sometimes but tried really hard. Campers came and went and with each one I gave lots of love, devotion and respect and they returned it.

In about the second week of July, I received my first pay check; it was $350.00. I was happy. I couldn't wait to cash my check. There was a bank in town that allowed us to cash our checks through them. There was also a bus that went into town so we could go shopping; it waited for us about an hour and a half. I already knew what, where, and how I was going to spend my money.

Jessica, Brenda, Shaquisha, Roberta and I hung out together after we cashed our checks. Jessica and I liked the same types of clothes. We bought some short sets, jeans and shirts, either the same or similar in style or color. Jessica also talked me into buying a perm for my hair. I never had a perm before. I told her horror stories of girls going bald, but she reassured me she knew what she was doing. As we left the store Jessica asked me to go window shopping with her because the other girls were still shopping. She was bored and was ready to go. We walked a couple of blocks, stopping every now and then to point at outfits or things in the window when I got the feeling we were being watched. I glanced around but didn't see anyone. Jessica was still chatting when I noticed an old maroon car in which sat two guys, staring at us. I got nervous and a little curious as to why they were sitting there smirking and staring. I nudged Jessica. "Don't turn around but directly behind us are two guys sitting there staring at us," I whispered. "Where?" she turned around quickly. "Oh," she said. I turned around to go but she just stood there. The driver of the car gestured for her to come over. Jessica left me. As she leaned on the passenger side talking, the passenger stared at me. I quickly looked away. Suddenly Jessica got in the car. She didn't even know the guys!

"Come on. Grace," she called.

I refused.

"Ah, come on," the guy on the passenger side urged.

I shook my head, "No."

"Besides you gotta come," one of the guys said.

"Why?" I asked. What did he mean, I don't have to do anything.

"We have your friend and you don't want her here by herself, do you?"

I thought about it for a moment and concluded that two was better than one. Who was I kidding? They were guys and we were girls. *If they attacked us, what was I going to do - beat them to death with a box of perm?*

"Come on, Grace," he coaxed.

Great, he knew my name. At least I won't die a Jane Doe.

"All right," I finally said. But, first, let us let our friends know we are going back to camp with you guys. We are going back to camp right?"

"Right! Sure!" they said in unison.

The passenger got out of the car, pushed the front seat forward, and waited politely for me to get in. As I was getting in he gave me a little bow, took me by the hand and assisted me further in the car. We stopped by the store and told the other girls we were catching a ride back to camp with some friends. Everyone wanted to know with whom but I told them I'd tell them later.

I was very quiet. I only answered questions when they were directed to me. The driver introduced himself as Marcus, and the passenger's name was James. Jessica and Marcus were in deep conversation. James turned around and talked with me. He was from Queens and worked up here with his friend Marcus who got him the job every summer. He also told me the job paid well. The nineteen year old still lived with his family, had graduated from high school, and was just enjoying life. He asked me about myself. I told him I was sixteen, from Brooklyn, worked as a counselor for the handicapped, and loved my job.

He applauded me. I liked James; he was nice looking, brown-skinned, and had big eyes that seemed very honest. He gave me the number to his job and the place where he was staying. I could call anytime, whether to talk or just hang out. I didn't have a phone and he understood. We said good-bye and left.

That night in the cabin the events were played out and Jessica got the same speech I did. We were not to get in cars with strangers. As weeks went by I didn't call James. Then one day Jessica suggested that we do. A few days later, I did.

"Layers of Lace"

It was my day off so I went early in the morning into the lunch room. No one was there because counselors were still getting their campers up. I called James. A groggy voice answered after several rings. I identified who I was and asked to speak to James. It sounded like the phone was dropped on the floor and after several long minutes another groggy voice answered. I knew instantly it was James. I said, "Hi, this is Grace; do you remember me?" There was a moment of silence and I wondered if I had made a mistake by calling him.

"James, are you there?" I asked.

"Yeah, I'm here."

"Did I call you at a bad time?"

"Nah," then he let out a sigh.

"Okay. Ah - maybe I'll call you later," I said.

"No, no it's all right. I'm just surprised you called me."

I was stumped.

"Grace?"

"Ah - yeah, I'm here. I only called cause you asked me."

"Nah, nah it's all right. I just didn't think you wanted to be bothered that's all. I mean I did wait for your call. I'd have waited another few weeks just as long as you called. Who could forget being in the presence of an angel?" I laughed.

"What's up? What ya doing today?" he asked.

"Oh yeah, that's why I called. I'm off the whole day and I wanted to know if you wanted to hang out?"

He had to work that day but was off on Saturday. I was really disappointed.

"Hold on, let me see something. I'll be right back," I said. I dropped a few coins in the phone. I was running out of change. "Don't hang up, okay?" I said.

"You kidding? I'm not hanging up for nobody. Go ahead, do what you gotta do," he answered.

I ran across the lunch room to where the schedules were posted and skimmed down to my name and across to Saturday. I was off. I skimmed to Jessica's name across and found she was off too. I ran back to the phone.

"James, James you there?"

"Yeah, I'm still here, Grace. What's up?"

"I'm off on Saturday and Jessica is too. Maybe she and Marcus can hang out with us. Ask Marcus and I'll ask Jessica okay?"

"All right, so it's a date?"

"Yup, it's a date," I said, excitedly.

He let out a yell. I heard muffled voices.

"See you Saturday?" he whispered.

"Okay. Bye James."

I danced a little step and started twitching my butt.

"Oh, yeah baby! Shake that stuff!" someone encouraged.

I whirled around and the cook, whom I forgot was there, laughed at me. I laughed back, waved, and ran out the door. I sped toward Jessica's cabin and came to a halt. I forgot she was seeing someone. She had met a guy who was also a counselor and they seemed pretty involved. I couldn't call James back. I didn't want his friends screaming on me. Later, I'd sort that out.

Camp seemed deserted. I wanted to go swimming, so I rushed to my cabin and changed into my bathing suit. I didn't wear a swimming cap. Jessica had permed my hair and it was straight. I loved it and I loved getting it wet because it looked even straighter, like white people's hair.

The thick hair hung past my shoulders. We were allowed to go swimming if there was a lifeguard. There was one on duty and there were also a few people swimming in the pool. One of them was Brenda, whom I knew already, two guys and another girl. I waved and kept going.

"Hey Grace, come in," Brenda called out.

"I'm coming. I just want to get used to the water first."

"Oh, I can get you used to some water now, right guys?" Brenda said looking as if she was about to splash me. Her friends followed her, smiling openly like they were ready to fire away as soon as she gave the command.

"You better not," I yelled. "I'll leave, I mean it!"

"Calm down. We won't splash you but as soon as you get in come over and tell us about James."

How did she know? Oh Right, Jessica was her roommate. I sat there dangling my feet and calves in the water. I partially submerged into the water. Slowly, I walked around then went completely under. I swam from one end to the other and came up again. As I grabbed hold of the edge of the pool someone thrust a towel at me. I looked at the towel and then the person. It was James!

"What are you doing here?" I gasped.

"I came to see you," he replied, smiling.

"But I thought you were working today?" I started climbing out of the pool.

He reached down and grabbed my arm, opened up the towel, and wrapped it around me.

"I was but I asked the boss for the day off. Things aren't too busy at the restaurant."

He leaned over and kissed me on the cheek. Someone giggled. It was Brenda. All the others were watching and smiling at me. I steered James toward the bench to sit down.

"How did you get up here?" I questioned.

"I drove."

"You drove?"

"Yeah, Marcus lent me the car. So get dressed and I'll take you to get something to eat, but first I want to take you to my job and introduce you to my friends. Is that all right with you?"

"Yeah, it's okay." I was smiling from ear to ear. "I'll be right back," I said, barely suppressing a giggle.

"Can I have some privacy people?" I yelled to the onlookers. I looked back at James and instructed over my shoulder, "Don't you go nowhere!" James threw both hands up in surrender. "I'm not going nowhere; I promise!" I ran back to the cabin and got dressed. I didn't wear as much make-up then as I had in the ninth grade. I looked in the mirror, pleased, and hurried back to James. He was still sitting there patiently. Brenda and the others were gone and the lifeguard was putting on sunscreen. I grabbed James' hand, waved good-bye to the lifeguard, and we left.

James complimented me on my appearance. He looked well, too. We went to the restaurant and introduced me to his friends. They were giving him fives, slaps on the back, and thumbs up signs. As we were leaving James whispered in my ear, "I told you, you are pretty."

James and I were inseparable the whole summer. Any time we had days off we were together. He even met some of my campers.

As my job came to an end I received my last paycheck, which I decided to save. I knew I would need new clothes for September. That morning I went to Shirley's office and asked if I could call my social worker. I called Mrs. Bogan only to find out she wasn't there anymore. In Manhattan someone named Mr. Bannings would meet me. I demanded to know what happened to Mrs. Bogan, but they were not allowed to discuss it. I wouldn't hang up; I sat and sobbed.

"Honey, listen, Mrs. Bogan is retired. She didn't want you to know. She knew you would take it hard but promised to keep in touch. Okay?"

"Yes," I responded. As I left Shirley's office, wiping my eyes, James was there waiting for me.

"Hi. What's wrong?" he asked. "Who's messing with you, where they at?"

I laughed. He was such an actor. I told him what happened. "Now listen Grace, here is my number and address in Queens. Don't lose it. And here is a picture, Okay? Don't lose it."

He gave me a tight hug and kissed the top of my head. I hugged him more tightly. I didn't want to let him go but I had to. The bus was pulling in. That was the saddest day of my life. We walked back to the cabin holding hands and he helped me gather my things. My bags seemed heavier.

"What's up with showing people my legs?" James gripped.

"Huh?" I snapped out of my daydream. I looked down. I had on a pair of short shorts, a striped tee shirt, and a pair of sneakers with white bootie socks.

"I didn't mean to," I started.

"It's all right; I'm kidding. You have nice big legs." James wrapped his arm around my shoulder.

I chose to ride the last bus and sat alone. As the bus pulled off I waved until I couldn't see James anymore. A few moments later I heard a horn beeping at me. It was James. We continued to wave but the bus out drove him. It felt good to have a person care so much about me.

I rode the bus in silence all the way back to Manhattan. When we finally arrived, I said my good-byes to all the people I met over the summer and ran over to Brenda. I gave her a big hug.

Chapter 4

A Few Wrinkles

As everyone cleared out, I stood alone on the sidewalk and waited for Mr. Bannings. I watched the cars, the people, even a dog or two walk by. Everyone was in a hurry. They knew where they were going, but I didn't. I was both scared and a little excited.

Someone calling my name snapped me from my deep thought. It was a tall, very handsome man standing before me.

"Excuse me, are you Grace Johnson?" This must have been Mr. Bannings.

"Yes, I am. Why?" I asked.

"I'm Mr. Bannings. I am to take you to Long Island. There is a car waiting. Please come with me." He reached over and took both my suitcase and bag. When I reached the car he opened the door. I climbed in, greeting the driver. Mr. Bannings loaded my baggage into the trunk and got into the car. Then we took off. I asked him if he knew Mrs. Bogan. He did. Mr. Bannings wasn't my social worker; he was only escorting me to Long Island. My social worker was a man named George Smith.

After about thirty minutes of conversation, I quieted down. We passed so many trees. I'd never been to Long Island and was very curious about my new family, too. They were the Jacobs. I hoped that they were nothing like my other four families because I was going to make it hell on earth for them if they were.

We reached our destination after a one hour drive. The traffic was very heavy. It seemed like the longest drive of my life. We arrived in front of a green-shingled, high ranch house. There were lots of flowers and plants. The lawn was well manicured and displayed statues.

"Oh Grace, Maxine is here also. I forgot to tell you." Mr. Bannings informed.

"Maxine?" I said loudly. "How? I mean how come?"

Mr. Bannings shrugged his shoulders and shook his head. I was glad to have someone here I knew.

We climbed some steps and Mr. Bannings rang the doorbell. After a few moments I heard someone approach the door, and it opened. A woman about my height answered. "Hello," she said in a raspy voice. "Come in." I extended my hands toward her. She nodded at me and shook my hand limply.

"Put those bags right there," she instructed and pointed to a spot by the door. She had claw-like fingernails. I didn't like her. She said we could sit in the living room, and she'd get us something to drink. As soon as she was out of sight I leaned over to Mr. Bannings and said, "I don't like her; she hates me."

"Now why would you say that, Grace?" he whispered.

"Didn't you see the way she looked and talked to me? I'm telling you she hates me!" I whispered desperately.

"Grace, listen, give it a chance. This is your fifth home, and you are sixteen. It's hard to place kids your age in homes. Please give it a chance, okay?"

I thought for a moment and nodded my head, but inside I was so unsure about the new arrangement.

Mrs. Jacobs finally returned with our sodas. I wondered if she put something in it. "Thank you. It's so hot today," Mr. Bannings said.

"Isn't it?" Mrs. Jacobs stated and let out a small raspy laugh. Her voice sounded like the mating ground of frogs.

"Mark!" she called out. "Mark! Come. Grace and Mr. Bannings are here." She didn't say much to me, but she talked to Mr. Bannings until a tall man appeared. He was smiling from ear to ear. "Oh, hello. How y'all doing?" His accent seemed southern.

Mr. Bannings got up quickly. "How you doing sir?" They shook hands. I got off the couch and shook hands with him too.

"Oh, hello." I liked him. As I turned to sit, I heard people laughing and talking downstairs. I glanced down and saw a familiar face heading up my way. "Grace!" Maxine called out and ran up the rest of the way to hug me. I was so happy. "Hey, Maxine. What's going on?" But Mrs. Jacobs quickly ended that reunion. "Go back downstairs Maxine, now." She pointed a claw downward. I looked over at Mr. Bannings, who gave me a weak smile and looked down.

After Maxine disappeared, I heard another set of feet heading upstairs. A tall, attractive girl was heading up. We exchanged smiles. "Hi," she said. It sounded as if she were singing.

"Hi," I said. "What's your ... " I started but was cut off again.

"Tracey," Mrs. Jacobs said, "I told y'all to stay downstairs; now go back downstairs." She left and I returned to the couch.

The bell rang and Mrs. Jacobs answered it. Mr. Jacobs and Mr. Bannings talked then. I was sulking when I heard a few voices saying, "Hi, Mommy." It was a mixture of male and female. Noisy feet ascended the steps. A woman greeted us. She shook my hand, smiled, and introduced herself as Evelyn.

"You must be Grace."

I answered. I liked her right away. A heavy-set guy introduced himself as Kirk. Two other men, Gary and Darrell, introduced themselves. I recognized Darrell from a picture on Mrs. Jacobs' wall. The caption read Dynamite Rhythms. He and his brother Kirk were in the music business. Darrell had a record out, which was doing well. I was in a home where celebrities lived. After meeting Evelyn's husband Robert, and Mrs. Jacobs' other son Russell, and Scott, Mr. Bannings was ready to go. As I walked him outside, he reassured me that he would inform Mr. Smith of how I was feeling. He patted my hand, "Grace, please give it a chance, okay?" I would try.

"The Lie"

As I re-entered the house, my heart felt very heavy. Mrs. Jacobs was waiting for me at the top stairs. I stood there for what seemed like eternity before she spoke.

"There are some things I will not tolerate in my house. I'm gonna set the record straight."

"All right," I said.

"I will not tolerate lesbian or anything like that in my house."

I wasn't sure what she was talking about.

"All right," I agreed.

"I will not permit you to ride Maxine or hump her anymore, or bully, hurt, or torment her either. Do you understand?"

"Huh?" My mind was in a whirl.

"Do you understand? Am I making myself clear?" Mrs. Jacobs was waiting for an answer.

"I don't understand," I told her. "What is this all about?"

"You know. She said you would play like you didn't know anything."

"She? Who is she?" I asked, puzzled.

"Maxine. She said how you tried to rape her and force her to do all these sexual acts on her. She is very afraid of you."

Mrs. Jacobs' eyes were like pointers. I didn't know what to say. And another thing, you will stay away from her. If I hear otherwise you are outta here."

Mrs. Jacobs never raised her voice even a notch.

"Mrs. Jacobs," I forced, "I never hurt Maxine, no not ever. I don't know what's going on, but what she told you is a lie. If you don't believe me, call Mr. Bannings, Mrs. Bogan, whoever. They will vouch for me. But Maxine is lying."

"All right, if she is lying, why did they remove you from your last home and you were sent away?"

"It was for personal reasons. I had to deal with sexual situations and much more than you care to know, but it had nothing to do with Maxine. I am shocked to see her here and not my brothers. Trust me Mrs. Jacobs, she's lying to you," I defended.

Mrs. Jacobs was taken aback. "Come with me." We headed downstairs. As we climbed down the last of four steps, we entered into what looked like a den or family room. Everyone, including Mr. Jacobs, was down there.

"Turn off that TV, Russell," Mrs. Jacobs said. Once the TV was off she turned to Maxine, who was smiling from ear to ear. "Maxine, what did you tell me about Grace?"

"Huh? Oh yeah, um Grace," she said turning toward me still smiling. "Um, remember when you did something to me? Remember?" she insisted.

"What are you talking about?" I asked.

"Remember?"

"No, I don't."

"When you tried to make me sleep with you?"

I was ticked off. "No, what I remember is you doing that to Mrs. C's daughter. I caught you two. Do you remember?" I smirked.

The grin disappeared from Maxine's face. She gasped desperately, trying to gain hold of her lie.

"No!" I snapped. "I've been through enough in my life already and I'm not taking any crap from you! Or nobody else! I will call Mrs. C up right now!"

"No, no don't," Maxine begged.

"Well, tell these people the truth."

By now everyone was all ears, waiting for the truth. Mrs. Jacobs stepped in.

"Maxine," she said very calmly. "Is what Grace saying true?"

"Yes, Mommy."

Mommy? What was up with that? Everybody started talking at once to Maxine.

"Why you say something like that?" someone questioned.

"I wanted everyone to like me," Maxine sadly said. Her head hung in shame.

"Oh man, like you? So you lied on Grace?" Tracey yelled. Her voice sounded like she was singing again.

"Yes, I'm sorry everyone," Maxine's eyes overflowed with tears. No one bought her act. Maxine could turn tears on as quickly as she turned them off.

"I'm sorry, Grace," Mrs. Jacobs softened her voice. "I misjudged you and I'm sorry." "Yeah," everyone said at once, only to re-badger Maxine.

I didn't feel sorry for her. I ran to my bag and pulled out a picture of James.

"This is my boyfriend James," I showed them. "Oh, he's handsome," Mrs. Jacobs said smiling. She handed me back the picture. "Grace, you hungry?" I was. "We got all this food set up at the table. Eat up," she urged. I grabbed a fork and Tracey gave me a plate, still smiling at me.

Mrs. Jacobs was one of the nicest people I ever met. Tracey, she and I were pretty close. But there was a thorn in my flesh which bore the name Maxine.

"Life Outside the Fence"

Before the summer ended, I asked Mrs. Jacobs if she could take me shopping. I had about three hundred dollars. I racked up on shoes, black jeans, shirts, school supplies, and personal items. I even bought another perm for my hair.

One day I was sitting outside on Mrs. Jacobs' front step, watching the cars and people go by. Mrs. Jacobs came to the front door. "Grace, I've been watching you for several weeks now. Why don't you go for a walk or something? You sit on those steps day in and day out."

"I can go outside the yard?" I asked.

"What? Are you kidding me? Yeah, go for a walk, girl. What you sitting there for?"

"I didn't think you would let me leave the yard. We weren't allowed to in my other foster homes." Mrs. Jacobs' jaw went limp.

"No child, get up from there and go," she insisted.

"Where can I go?"

Mrs. Jacobs shrugged her shoulders.

"Go anywhere but here."

"Ooo! Can I go with Grace?" Maxine begged.

Before I could object, Mrs. Jacobs did it for me.

"Let Grace alone; now go ahead Grace. I'll see you later." She shooed Maxine upstairs and disappeared.

It was too good to be true. I could walk out the front yard and go anywhere I pleased. I started walking west but changed my mind. I walked around the corner, then up the street, past the high school I would be attending in September, a supermarket, post office, and a library. I must have walked about two miles or more. It was exhilarating.

In September I began to attend Brentwood Ross High School. I walked to school with Russell and Scott. We were pretty cool together but Russell was very quiet, while Scott was a talker. Scott thought he knew everything. Russell was handsome, with long hair that he kept braided all the time. He loved to draw and was really good. He also loved to rap and write music. I tried to get him to open up to me but he wasn't much of a talker.

At school I went to the front office where they gave me my schedule. Filling out the forms made me late to my first period class – gym.

When I entered, everyone was sitting on bleachers. It seemed like these bleachers went on for miles and were loaded with teenagers. They were all shades, sizes, and colors. I pushed past my nervousness and located a spot on the bleachers in the far front end, away from everyone. The back was really my preference. As the gym teachers quieted us down, I saw the chatterers, loners (like me), comedians, a few rockers, and one person who stood out. It was a girl who looked very young, attractive and also bounced when she walked. She had extraordinary hair. When she looked left her hair swung left. If she looked right it swung right. Even at the slightest movement her hair swung. I watched her as her name was being called. She laughed and talked with some other girls who sat next to her. She had a nice smile and the straightest, whitest teeth I ever saw. I wondered if they were fake. Still she had a nice smile. I looked away because my name was called. I got up and began walking across the gym floor. I suddenly felt very self-conscious, like everyone was watching me. I got my locker number and sat back in my secluded spot. I don't remember how long I sat but I heard someone saying, "Hi." I was scribbling my name across the front cover of my notebook. I looked up to see the long-haired girl sitting next to me.

"Oh, hi," I replied.

"I'm Chris, Chris Long."

Chris? What kind of name is that for a girl, I thought to myself.

"Mine is Grace."

"You must be new here."

"Yup. I'm from Brooklyn, New York."

"Oh yeah? I have family out there."

Out there? She made it sound like another planet.

"Yeah? What part?"

"They live in Bushwick. You know where that's at?"

"Uh-huh, Brooklyn. I'm just kiddin'," I laughed. She didn't.

People often found me strange because I would say things that didn't always flow with the conversation. I knew what I was saying; it's just that others didn't. From the days of my youth I remember going to see psychiatrists because my foster parents and social workers didn't believe I was all there.

I didn't want to lose my newfound friend so I quickly asked her what classes she was in. I wanted to see whether we had any of the same classes. The bell rang and I got up to leave.

"Wait I'll walk you. Mine is on the way."

"Oh, all right," I said. We immediately became friends.

"Speaking Our Minds"

Chris' sister Leslie and I shared two classes. Leslie was cool but she knew how to push buttons. Her best friend at the time, Annette Jones, held mean expressions. She would squint her eyes and mouth so tightly that she looked angry all the time. Chris loved her, but I didn't. I was afraid of her. Leslie, on the other hand, was a comic. She was as skinny as a rail, with freckles all over her face, and had thick brownish red hair. She didn't look like she got much sun. Leslie was also loud. Every lunch period you heard her then saw her. I liked sitting with her.

One day Leslie and I got into a disagreement. She always bragged about a guy she dated named Raymond Murphy. I didn't have a boyfriend for I had lost James' phone number and through the months lost touch with him. So I bragged about Dynamite Rhythms. I would say things like "You know Dynamite Rhythms? Their record went gold and they are my cousins." After a while Leslie said, "Oh, they are played out. They didn't make anything after that."

"So what's it to you? At least they made a record," I shot back.

By then people began to turn around or look over because Leslie was so loud. I got a couple of nods of agreement.

"Yeah, but Run-DMC is better than them and plus their record went platinum," Leslie pushed.

There were a few nods for Leslie. I gasped.

"Yeah, well they are touring with Run-DMC and they are down with one another," I offered.

"But they only made one song; it's old and it's played. You can't compare them because Run-DMC is number one on the billboard. Where are your cousins? Oops, they are no where to be found! What now, Grace? What now?"

By then Leslie was talking so loudly that it sounded like she was screaming.

"All right, calm down. Stop yelling at me."

I hated scenes and Leslie reminded me of Diana so much. After that argument, Leslie and I didn't talk for weeks.

"Waves of Music"

One particular day I was sitting in the lunchroom when I heard some guys banging on a table. One of them appeared to be chanting while two others banged. I leaned forward slightly to get a piece of the rhyme. The vocalist was Craig Mack from my math class. He sat behind me and constantly wrote. His writing had nothing to do with math. Craig sported a low afro, was approachable, and had a great personality. Craig could free style (make rhymes up without writing them down) very well. Eric Sermon, was not only a rapper, but a clown. He could make anybody laugh. He was very friendly and popular. These two, along with others, had battles going on and would get people across the lunch room nodding their heads in unison. That ignited the music in me. I wanted to rap again, too.

When I was about fourteen, my brother Anthony had pushed me to enter a rap contest at a block party. So I entered it. When the D.J. gave me the microphone and asked me my name, I said boldly, "Lady M.C."

"Yo, yo everyone listen up; we got Lady M.C. in the house!" he announced over a big microphone. That brought a crowd. When I saw them, I got so scared that my hands started shaking and sweating. He smiled and urged me on. The D.J. played a fast beat that didn't go with what I was saying and it threw me off further. My heart was sprinting by then. I was booed, yelled at, and would have had garbage cans thrown at me if some hadn't been tied down. Never again did I, or would I, embarrass myself. But in secret I would write many rap lyrics with me as my audience. Craig and I became great friends. I would meet him in the halls or in math class. "So Craig," I would say, "what you do over the weekend?"

"Oh, I went to the recording studio to cut a record." Or he'd hung out with some famous rap artist. I was amazed. "Stop lying Craig," everyone in class would object.

"A Different Shade"

One day I caught Maxine putting bread with butter in the toaster. When I confronted her, she lied. We argued for a while then I raised my hand and shoved her head. This pitched us into a scuffle. I pounded her head, punched her in the face, and then put her in a headlock. I was filled with so much rage because I didn't like Maxine and I wanted to release all I was feeling inside. Human contact in any physical form would do. That commotion brought Russell, Mrs. Jacobs, Tracey and Scott from their bedrooms. When Russell pushed me off Maxine, my rage shifted to him. He returned his anger with equal vengeance. We were two teenagers who had different personalities, and we hated each other. As Russell swung on me Scott grabbed me. I reached for Mrs. Jacobs' vase on the table. She snatched it out my hand before I could bring it down on her son's head. Mrs. Jacobs never broke up any fights; she felt we should just release it and get it out our system. Scott threw me on the floor and shielded me. I screamed at the top of my lungs. Russell was still swinging and Scott caught every blow in his face. Russell was blind to the fact that he was hitting his brother instead of me. I tried to scramble from under Scott but as I stuck my head from under his shield, I caught a blow to my eye. It was the same eye I had received a football, which was thrown by my brother Anthony who was playing with it in the house after my Grandma (Mrs. Evans) told him not to. It was the same eye that caught a blow from a baseball also thrown by one of my brothers. And yes! The same eye that received many a blow from Mrs. Evans when I ticked her off. Now here it is eighteen years later receiving another blow from a fist of a madman.

Mrs. Jacobs stepped in and broke up the fight. She sent Russell downstairs in the den to cool off and kneeled beside Scott and me to talk.

"Grace," she said. "Are you all right?"

"No!" I yelled.

"Calm down Grace, stop yelling."

"No! I won't! You are not right," I accused. "You always take up for Russell because he's yours and Scott and I aren't," I cried out.

"Now you know that isn't true. I always listen to all you kids; I love you all the same."

Scott got up slowly, obviously in extreme pain. I scrambled and tried to help him but he waved me away. I didn't speak to Mrs. Jacobs nor Russell for many days after that.

Chapter 5

College Days

After graduation from Brentwood Ross High School I was accepted at Dowling College in Oakdale, Long Island. I was accepted into a program called HEOP and lived on campus. I was doing fairly. I met lots of friends, and I got involved in many sexual relationships that none of my friends knew about.

I still called Chris occasionally; we were best friends. I would hang out with her over the weekend. Chris and I kept jobs and money. We both liked clothes, hanging out, and men. Chris was very particular about whom she dated. She was into looks. But I had a preference for dark guys. While Chris often got her heart broken, I did the heartbreaking. I refused to let anyone hurt me or get too close.

I took a theater course in college. I wanted to act because it gave me an opportunity to disguise myself. I also pursued modeling. I never took it seriously, but inside I wanted to be one. There were so many things going against me: I was too short, and had a slight over bite. I never really pushed myself to do much of anything.

Dowling College was pretty straight laced, but for me life was descending into a slow spiral. One day I got approved for a student loan. I then received a check which I cashed. I called Chris up and agreed to meet her in Brentwood. From there we took a train to Brooklyn. We met at her brother Matthew's house. He took Chris and me to Delancey Street in Manhattan because he felt we could get more clothes for our money. I bought a leather coat with a fur collar and one for Chris. My coat had white smooth fur; Chris' coat had fur that fanned her face. She constantly had to keep shoving it away. "Let's trade coats," she kept insisting.

"Nope! Nope!" I kept saying. "I picked this one out first." I bought jeans and shoes and treated my best friend. After shopping we went back to Matthew's house and changed into our new outfits. A few hours later Chris and I walked around the neighborhood. As we were turning around to head back to Matthew's house, we passed two guys who appeared to be just standing around.

"What's up" one of them piped up. Chris and I said, "Hi," and kept on walking.

"Yo, what's your name?" he pursued. I turned around and headed toward them with Chris in tow. "What's your name?" the guy repeated.

"I'm Grace and this is Chris," I said. "What's yours?"

"Mine is Paul, and this is Cash," he answered.

"Cash? What type of a name is that?" I asked.

He shrugged and laughed.

"Where you two heading?" Paul pressed.

"I'm going to Chris' brother's house down the street here."

"Well, why don't you two chill with us?" Paul asked.

Chris and I both agreed. We laughed and talked for hours. Chris liked Cash and I fell head over heels for Paul. He was funny, attractive, and liked attention. I felt very comfortable being around him. He liked the fact of someone going to college. He asked Chris why she didn't go. I answered and said, "She didn't graduate, that's why."

Chris frowned and folded her arms across her chest. She was angry.

"What? You kiddin' me. Why you didn't graduate? I mean I didn't either, I dropped out, but still you should have finished," Paul probed.

I volunteered that Chris dropped out to get a job at Country Fried Chicken. Paul burst out laughing and so did Cash. They slapped fives.

"Word," they kept saying. I laughed.

Chris was upset so she walked off. I didn't see the pain I caused her. I was becoming more self-centered. I said good-bye to Paul and Cash. I ran to catch up with Chris and apologized. She didn't say anything, but by the time we reached Matthew's house we were talking like nothing happened.

"Stained Material"

In just a few weeks Paul and I were steadily seeing each other. I became very sick and was tired all the time. I could hardly sit in my classes and at times couldn't even make it to class. I was contemplating dropping out. A visit with the doctor proved I was pregnant. I was filled with untold terror. I didn't know who the father was and Paul immediately denied the baby was his. He told me, however, whatever decision I made, he would stand by me. I loved him even more for that.

In February of 1988, I decided to drop out of college. Paul tried to talk me out of it, but I insisted I would return to school in the future. I also decided not to keep the baby. I was eighteen years old, with no job and no school. Paul stood by me. Mrs. Jacobs said I could come back home. I told her about the pregnancy and that I wanted an abortion. She didn't judge me or lecture me, but supported me. She never mentioned it again.

I began accompanying Paul to Wyandanch, Long Island, where he lived with a friend. This friend also shared space with a brother-in-law and five sisters.

On some of my visits I would witness these family members break out in fist fights and arguments. Paul and I didn't pay them any mind. We were used to stuff like that. Russell and I had engaged in fist fights at Mrs. Jacob's house. So when I saw these things go on with Paul's friend's family members, it didn't phase me.

"Circle of Trouble"

One day Paul was drinking heavily and we got into an argument. Later, he left with Bill to go to a party. So when Bill's sister Lydia suggested that we go to a party also, I agreed. Paul had run out to a party and I felt two can play that game.

The party wasn't really crowded but I got a lot of stares from girls who were curious about "the new chick" stepping on their turf. I also got stares from guys. I became a wallflower. Lydia already knew the fierce looking females, but I didn't. I really didn't care to. Suddenly I saw Paul across the room with Bill. He was standing with his arms folded across his chest, and his eyes locked on me like an eagle in pursuit of its prey. I was filled with terror. Paul stepped up to Lydia and whispered in her ear. She turned, walked up to me, and told me that Paul wanted her to take me home.

"I'm not going home," I revolted.

"Come on, Grace," she called as she walked out of the door. Then she returned and took my arm.

"Let's go, Grace. Paul wants you at the house, so let's go." I snatched my arm away.

"I'll go when I get ready," I said.

"You don't know Paul, it's best you go," she insisted.

"What do you mean?" I asked.

"Never mind that, let's go now!"

I was curious and tried to pressure her into telling me what she meant when Paul walked up and grabbed my arm.

"Go home now," he hissed.

His eyes penetrated mine like a surge of fire. I was terrified.

"Go," he commanded.

Heads turned as people began staring and whispering. With my legs feeling like watery stilts, I headed out the door toward the house. That night after Paul returned to the house, drunk, he behaved as though he didn't remember. After seeing Paul for several months I hadn't seen how mean and cruel he could be; maybe I just didn't want to.

*****

A few weeks after my abortion, the nurse told me that my period would not be regular for a few months, but that I could resume my regular activities. I went shopping with Lydia and her friends. We walked down a long street called Straight Path, which led to a chain of stores and clusters of guys hanging out. This was the real reason they wanted to hit this spot – to meet guys. I was wearing beige pants and a sky blue top. My clothes were tight fitting, a trend I had developed and stuck with since high school. I was a real Janet Jackson fan then, so I copied Janet's preference for black pants and an earring with a key.

Off I went with my Janet Jackson hairstyle, wearing eyeliner and lipstick as my only make-up. We walked around for about fifteen minutes. Lydia and the other girls waved and talked to people they knew. We had to keep stopping and waiting for someone in the group to finish their long conversations about who's going with whom or who's in jail. I began to feel moisture between my legs, but it didn't concern me. I always had some discharge. Then Lorraine came up beside me and whispered in my ear.

"Grace we have to get you home."

"How come?" I asked, puzzled.

"Because you have blood all over your pants in the back."

My heart beat so fast that I was short of breath. I became aware that everyone knew and was pointing and laughing. Lorraine gave me her sweater and I wrapped it around my waist. I looked around for Lydia, who was in deep conversation with a guy. She looked up and saw me. I signaled for us to go. She ignored me and kept on talking. Lydia's sister, Rachel, had just gotten off work so she walked me back to the house. Lorraine returned to Lydia's side in their manhunt. A few moments later, Lydia returned, not just with her sisters and Lorraine but with a bunch of other 40-oz.-drinking, I'll-take-your-man-chicks.

Paul was sitting in the living room when they came in. I didn't tell him what had happened to me. But one of them did. I leaned against the door to the bathroom which was just across the hall from the living room. I heard Paul saying in a low voice, "What?"

"Yeah," one of the girls was whispering.

I couldn't make out what she was saying to him.

"ELL," Paul yelled. "That's nasty! That b---- better not try to get none tonight. She might give me AIDS even if I wear a condom!"

The girls burst out in hysterical laughing. That only egged Paul on.

"Yeah, she better not be trying to get none of my big stuff, man. I'm Mr. Paul from Brooklyn! Yeah boy!"

There was more hysterical laughing and clapping of hands and more cruel jokes from Paul of Brooklyn. Through the chaos I heard Rachel's sweet voice saying, "Don't say that. She loves you and you shouldn't treat her so cruel. She is a very nice, sweet girl. "She's a good girl." Rachel was defending me the best way she could, but Paul ignored her and kept belittling me. The heart that I gave him many months before was crushed. I heard a soft knock at the bathroom door and hesitated. I didn't know if this was a prank that Paul wanted to play out so he could get props from the girls. Again the knock sounded. I opened the door slowly and peeked out. Rachel smiled.

"Grace, can I come in?"

I nodded my head and opened the door wide enough for just her frame to fit in.

"Here are some clothes I got out of your overnight bag."

"Thank you," I said, avoiding eye contact, in a voice that was barely a whisper.

The tears began to flow and I couldn't stop them. Rachel pulled me to her and embraced me. "Ssh," she said. "It's all right; it's all right. Girl, you hold your head up. Forget Paul. He's stupid;

that's all." I nodded and pulled away from her. She left to give me privacy. After I washed up, got dressed, and gathered my stuff, I exited the bathroom. Holding my head up, I took a deep breath and entered the living room. Paul was in the middle of telling another joke. He quickly swallowed it and sat down without saying a word. I must have looked like a terrifying sight, standing there with my bloody clothes in a ball. I got an image of how Carrie looked when they dropped pig's blood on her. The girls must have read my countenance and heard my thoughts because not one of them said a word or looked my way. It was very quiet. I could almost hear their breathing stop. Paul tried to say something but changed his mind when he looked at my face. I stuffed my clothes in a bag and left the house. Life with him was the beginning of many sorrows.

*****

In June of 1988, I got pregnant again. I was scared to tell Paul. A few weeks after the incident, Paul asked me to live with him. I was so in love with him. All he had to do was give me some of that sweet talking, layer it with apologies, and I would forgive him every time. I knew I had to tell Paul that I was pregnant. So a few days after Wyandanch Day, I told him. He had come home from work tired and wanted to get some rest. I followed him to the room. He sat on the edge of the bed and began pulling off work boots and clothes. I helped him and then I laid the news on him. He sat there and stared at me. Paul put his hands on his head and rested his elbows on his knees. I was still kneeling at his feet just, looking at him.

"Paul," I pushed, "tell me what you're thinking?"

"I don't know. I don't know. This is a mess," he said.

"A mess? How's that?" I asked. He let out a long sigh.

"You know Victoria, my ex in the city?" I remembered her. "She's pregnant, too," he continued.

"Well, how is that a mess for you?" I questioned.

"It just is."

"What ya mean, Paul?"

"She's pregnant by me, Grace. You should have known that, Grace. That's all."

"Me? I should have known? You should have told me!" I snapped. "Besides you two broke up a while ago, before me. That's what you told me!"

By then I was rising off my knees, but my eyes never left his face.

"Well, she is," Paul spouted.

"How far is she?"

"A month or two is all she said."

"A month or two," I yelled. "When were you going to tell me, huh? Wait hold up. A month or two! That means you were dealing with us both at the same time!!" I was really yelling.

"Shut up! Grace, I mean it!"

"No!" I continued. "You're not my father! When were you going to tell me!"

Paul jumped up, enraged, and grabbed me by the throat.

"Shut up," he said through clinched teeth. "Shut the f--- up or else I'll kill you!"

I was filled with terror as my lungs strained for air. I tried to pry his hands off my throat but that only made him use both hands to tighten the hold. When he let go of me I fell to my knees, gasping for air.

"Don't you ever question me again! Do you understand?" He punched me in my face. I laid on the floor and just cried. I didn't challenge Paul about any of his business again.

As always, days went by and Paul dismissed the incident. But I never forgot. There were several times during my pregnancy that Paul would break out in those rages and would pounce on me. Whenever my face was battered or my lip was puffed out, I would stay inside. I would later call Mrs. Jacobs to tell her what was going on.

"Come home, Grace. Please come home; you know you're always welcome," she told me.

"I know. Thanks," was all I managed.

"Grace listen, you are pregnant. You shouldn't go through these episodes of continuous beatings like that. You have to think of that baby you are carrying."

"All right Ma," I promised, and then I would hang up.

After waking from drunken sleep Paul would then deliver a kick in my back that sent me flying into a wall, or he'd chase me down the street, catch me and whip me before I could reach the train station. He'd drag me by my hair. If ever I tried to hit him with my umbrella, or anything I had in my hand, he would snatch it and beat me with it. Then he would pull me all the way back to the house.

"Ragged Seams"

I befriended a woman named Mrs. Seymour who worked at the Wyandanch Clinic. She was a nurse there and I trusted her. She saw my battered face, eyes, and swelling belly. She was very angry with Paul and tried many times to get me to leave him. But I just couldn't. I felt there was something I did or said that justified his anger. Mrs. Seymour insisted that the problem wasn't me; it was Paul. I defended him and left her office.

Paul had a habit of giving me twenty dollars on Fridays, paying the rent, and disappearing until Sunday. I didn't question him, but encouraged him to go. He was always so stressed out and uptight that I felt hanging out was good for him. He reassured me that all he did was hang-out with his boys, smoke weed, and drink. He did this for several months. As time went by and the fighting progressed, I moved back into Mrs. Jacob's house, temporarily. A few months later, I returned to Brooklyn and rented a large room in Bed-Stuy from Evelyn for $350. The room was furnished and had a sink, but I shared the kitchen and bathroom with other tenants. I paid my monthly rent of $350 with money I received from the Department of Social Services. I felt lonely. I took walks around the neighborhood and often sat in my room doing nothing at all. I could feel the life inside my womb nudge and kick me. I would trace my finger around the lump that would raise from within my belly, or tap it just to have it tap back. I read books on giving birth and how the baby looked inside the womb each month. I was seven months pregnant. Paul popped over to see me and spent some time with me. One day we both were sleeping on the bed when he jumped up.

"What's the matter?" I asked, startled.

"I'll be back," was all he said, and left.

A few hours later he returned with red eyes.

"Gimme twenty dollars, Grace." I gave him twenty dollars. He ran out the door and returned an hour or two later.

"Grace," he said, "Give me twenty dollars."

"What! I just gave you twenty Paul, you tripping!"

"Come on please, just give me the money!"

"What for?" I asked.

"Just gimme the blanking money," he hollered.

I quickly fetched out twenty and threw it at him across the bed. He looked like a dirty, rabid dog. I had a flashback of the Paul I didn't like. I quickly recovered and began unpacking the baby things I had bought that morning. I had just got my welfare check and had a hundred and odd dollars for savings. When Paul returned screaming for more money, I knew something wasn't right. His clothes were wet, and he was drenched from head to toe. "Gimme twenty dollars," he repeated.

"I said I didn't have anymore money."

"Look b----, don't lie to me!"

"I'm not lying," I insisted. "It's all gone. What's up with you Paul?"

"Mind your own business," he said.

He grabbed my purse and I folded my arms across my chest. As he was searching, he made small grunting sounds, jerking and throwing stuff around in my bag. I stared at him, noticing for the first time that his facial hair was dirty, overgrown, and he smelled a little. This was not the Paul I knew. He had been a handsome, well-groomed man who liked flashy clothes and jewelry. It was then I realized that he didn't wear his jewelry anymore.

"Where are your chains and stuff, Paul?"

"I pawned them," he said, still rummaging through my bag like a lunatic.

I was disheartened because he'd taken pride in those things. Paul eventually left without any more money.

Chapter 6

More Circles Added
1989

On March 12th, early in the morning, I asked Paul if I could go to Long Island and stay with him a few days. I wanted him to be around when the baby was born. He agreed but said that he wouldn't be home much because he was busy. I didn't mind. When I got to Wyandanch, Paul wasn't there to meet me. I took a cab to the house. Paul had gone out with Bill for several hours. I was fed up with him. A few hours later Paul and Bill returned. Paul was high as a kite. We made love that night. I woke up around ten o'clock in excruciating pain. I curled up in a ball and began to rock on my knees, moaning a little.

"What the ... ," Paul woke up, dazed. "What's wrong with you?" he asked.

"Paul, I'm in pain," I said with as much strength as I could. "Help me, it hurts."

"Oh, come on, I'm trying to get sleep," he snapped. "Shut up, will you? I'm tired."

I eased off the bed and headed toward the bathroom. I wanted to urinate but each step brought a shock of pain that blinded me. I doubled over and this time cried out.

"Grace!" Bill, this time, called out. "What's wrong?"

I said nothing. I inched to the bathroom and shut the door behind me. I left the lights off because I felt that light would only aggravate the pain. I welcomed the cool breeze coming through the open window. I sat down on the toilet and extinguished every ounce of water I believed my bladder could muster. I was relieved but the pain grew worse. I tried to return to my spot on the bed only to find Paul lying in my place. "Don't get back on this bed," Paul said. "You wanted to have this baby, so just deal with it." I was in too much pain to argue. I paced up and down along the foot of the bed. But in a few minutes I wound up in the bathroom releasing another ton of urine. "Paul," I cried out, "please help me." The pain was intensifying. Paul was silent. Bill's girlfriend called out into the darkness.

"Grace, do you need help?"

"Yes," I said.

"It's all right because I can deliver your baby if need be, okay?"

"Okay," I cried from the bathroom. *I had another week before delivery so that won't be an issue.*

When I emerged from the bathroom, the living room was lit up and Bill and his girlfriend were sitting on the couch with their coats on. She got up and stepped toward me. I steadied myself with my hand resting on the wall. Each step brought new pain. I asked Bill if he could take me home to Brentwood. He threw all my things in a bag and helped me to his car. Once inside he drove like a crazed man, thumping along railroad tracks. This introduced more pain, fiercer than the others.

When we finally got to Brentwood, Mrs. Jacobs was already waiting at the door. I said "good-bye" and "thanks" to my two heroes and headed toward the front door. I didn't tell Mrs. Jacobs I was in pain. I told her over the phone I wanted to come home so she thought I had a fight with Paul. I told her to go back to bed, because I was going downstairs in the den to watch TV. She returned to bed.

I laid across the couch, tossed and turned to stop the agony. I had to go to the bathroom again. This time I turned the lights on. After urinating my brains out I had a feeling to turn and look in the toilet. There was brown snottish stuff in the toilet and some on my underwear. I panicked and hurried to Mrs. Jacobs' room. I stood on her side of the bed and shook her gently. "Mommy," I whispered.

"What's the matter, Grace" she stirred.

"I'm in pain and I went to the bathroom to pee and saw this brown stuff in the toilet."

She sat up in the bed like a strike of lighting. She reached over and turned the light on.

"Are you sure?"

"Uh-huh. The books I read said my labor probably is starting, but it will be several weeks before the baby comes."

"Never mind those books."

She reached for the phone and called 9-1-1.

"Oh, come on," Mr. Jacobs said. "What time is it?" he asked. I looked at the clock; it read 11:15. "Girl! I got's to go to work in a couple hours. I need my sleep," he hollered.

"I'm sorry, Daddy," I said and remained quiet.

"Come on, Grace. I'll sit with you in the kitchen," Mrs. Jacobs encouraged.

Mrs. Jacobs sat across from me and stared. I sat quietly looking at my hands in my lap. The cops arrived and rang the bell. Mrs. Jacobs hurried to answer it. I heard them ask her who was in labor. Two police officers came up the stairs and I walked out the kitchen to meet them. They looked me over and asked if I was in labor.

"Yes," I said.

"When did it start?" I didn't know.

"Are you in pain now?" they continued.

"Yes," I said.

I saw uncertainty written all over their faces. They may have expected me to be screaming. The ambulance arrived a few moments later, and the police were dismissed.

I would have appreciated the ride under different circumstances but I didn't enjoy being bounced around. Some nurses were already waiting outside. I climbed off the stretcher into a wheelchair, in which the nurse whirled me through emergency room doors into a room with a bed, curtain and TV. I changed into a night gown, after which they examined me. I was seven centimeters. I was then transported from the first floor to the fifth or sixth floor and put in a birthing room. The nurse turned on the TV. Madonna was dancing and singing, "It's like a Prayer." The pain was becoming unbearable. A doctor entered the room and examined me.

"Why did you wait so long to come in, Grace?" I could tell from his accent that he was from the islands. "I don't know," was all I could say. He told the nurse to monitor me. I was happy to have her stay. I didn't want to be alone. I was afraid of the unknown. I heard muffled voices next to the wall that divided another room from mine. A woman was screaming and speaking another language. That sparked more fear in me. "What are they doing to her?" I asked the nurse. "Oh honey, she's having a baby like you." I asked the nurse why I wasn't screaming like her. "You know Grace, some people can't take pain." The nurse hurried for the door. "Wait," I cried out. "Where are you going?" I reached over and grabbed her hand. "Please don't go," I begged. I grasped her hand as tightly as I could, but she pried herself loose and reassured me that she would return.

Another nurse came in a few moments later and kept me company. I suddenly felt the urge to move my bowels. She spread some plastic sheets under me and directed me to go right there. Then she cleaned me up, removed the mess, and ran out of the room only to return with the doctor. He checked me. "She's ten, let's go," he commanded. "Grace, you're the best patient I ever had. I tell you, you're the best." I felt good. They pushed me down to the cold white delivery room. I had to put my legs in stirrups. The doctor changed into scrubs and put on a mask. He sat on a stool and urged, "Now! Grace, push!" I started pushing. I felt very awkward, like I wasn't doing it right. "Come on Grace, push, push harder." I let out a yell! "No Grace, no! Close your mouth; put your chin in your chest; and push!" I leaned forward and the nurses held my back up. "Push Grace, push. You can do it." They sounded like cheerleaders, so I pushed.

"Okay now, stop pushing." I felt the urge to keep pushing. It was so unbearable that I flowed with it. "No, Grace," the doctor yelled. "Don't push, just pant." I breathed rapidly. I wanted to get past the urge to push. "Now push again, Grace. *Would he make up his mind!* I felt my vagina stretching and then something plopped out of me. The baby was placed on my stomach. The nurse snatched him away, cleaned him up, and brought back an oval-shaped ball with a face. He was wearing a tiny hat. I reached for the baby.

"No, No, Grace," the nurse scolded. "Just look at him." I did. He was cute and was making smacking sounds with his mouth. "He's hungry," I told the nurse. "I know, honey. We will feed your son in a minute."

"Why are his eyes swollen?" I asked.

"That's some medicine we put in them to help him see better."

I was stitched up because I tore and was placed in my room to rest. They brought my son several times during the night. I felt odd feeding him. He was a good baby; he didn't cry. He just stared into my eyes as if he understood so much.

The next day Mrs. Jacobs and Evelyn came up to see me. I was happy to see them. "Grace," Mrs. Jacobs said, "That baby looks just like you, girl." I threw the covers back, put on my slippers and robe, and headed off to see my son. There were lots of babies. My son was lying toward the row in the back, sucking eagerly on a pacifier.

"Ma, of course he looks like me. He's the only black baby in there!"

"Really, I didn't notice," she replied, leaning into the glass.

We stood there laughing. I stood there watching them as they watched my son. Evelyn asked me his name. I didn't have one, for I was expecting a girl. She suggested "Tyrone." I pulled out his papers for his birth certificate.

*****

Tyrone was a very quiet and well-behaved baby. He didn't cry much. If you fed him, kept him dry and let him see you, you didn't hear him. Paul was overjoyed about our new baby.

Tyrone and I lived in Brooklyn for about six months. Paul and I were still off and on. One day I decided to go to church and attended one down the street from me. The people there were very friendly and treated me kindly. They told me if I needed anything I should visit them.

After I left church Paul was waiting at the house for me. I hadn't seen him for weeks at a time, and suddenly he appeared at the house after I decided to go to church. He wanted to know if I would like to move back in with him. I packed my bags and moved back to Wyandanch, Long Island. By that time Lydia and all her sisters had moved down south. Bill was seeing a new girl named Kathy, and all seemed to be going well.

Paul and Bill began throwing parties. There was a lot of drinking, smoking, cursing, and fighting. I had begun to drink. Bill told me that I was not a drinker.

"Why is that?" I asked.

"Because you don't sip beer; you have to guzzle it down. You waste it after a half of bottle."

I felt insulted. *How dare he say I'm not a drinker!* I decided to prove to him and everyone else that I was a drinker.

"A Few Needle Points"

When I became drunk, I was more funny. Paul, on the other hand, became more violent. It was like adding fuel to fire. The one who wound up hit usually was me. I began to fight back. Once I grabbed hold of a beer bottle and cut Paul in the head. I had also tried to stab him with a butcher knife. At times Bill would wrestle the knife out of my hand and Kathy would lead me to my room. I was getting fed up with the drama.

A rash developed over the left side of my nose. It itched badly and I scratched it until the skin became raw. Then my vision had become very blurred. I needed to see a doctor. I was diagnosed with second-stage syphilis. The nurse wanted me to go back to the clinic so they could do some more tests and I had to bring my mate with me. I had been down that road more than three or four times with Paul, and I didn't want to travel it again. I was contemplating leaving Paul for good. A year and a half of going down streets that only led to dead ends was becoming too much of a habit for me. I wanted to walk other streets, and I didn't want to see Paul on any of them.

When Paul came back from his rendezvous in Brooklyn, I told him about my session with the health nurse. "It's not me; you didn't get it from me," he kept saying. That Monday we went to the clinic. We met Mrs. Seymour. She called us into her office and proceeded to tell us what syphilis is and how it was contracted. I sat with Tyrone in my lap and listened attentively. Meanwhile, Paul was sighing, rolling his eyes, murmuring, and sucking his teeth. Mrs. Seymour stopped speaking and fastened her eyes on Paul.

"What is your problem?" she asked.

"Nothin' man, nothin'."

"What do you mean *nothin'*? This is a very serious situation," she said.

"Well, she didn't get it from me. That's my word," Paul said nastily.

"What do you mean she didn't?" Mrs. Seymour questioned. "How do you know that?"

"I'm not no hoe; she is. That's why," Paul snapped.

I nearly jumped out of my seat. *How dare he blame me!* Mrs. Seymour jumped in before I got a chance. She spoke in a voice that would crumble a nation.

"You listen to me and listen good. Don't be coming up in my office trying to out talk me because I tell you now, I will throw you out myself. Not only that, this child has been in here many a day with all types of sexual diseases."

She flung up my folder and slammed down papers from my file. She began reading off the contents one by one. Gonorrhea, not once but twice, chlamydia, what's next AIDS?" She then turned and asked me, "What's next Grace, AIDS?" I shook my head. "Well, you better leave him alone, wake up and go on with your life girl!" She glared at Paul who rolled his eyes and looked away. "Please leave my office now," she told him. Paul got up and waited for me to do the same. I gathered my things and Tyrone, but Mrs. Seymour restrained me. "You, you go," she said to Paul, pointing him toward the door. Paul was not happy when he left.

"You all right?" Mrs. Seymour asked me.

"Yes."

"You gonna be all right?" she asked.

"Yes."

"Okay, here are some numbers of people who can help you or if you just want to talk."

I thanked her and left.

*****

After that incident Paul began beating on me again. A few months earlier the doctor warned me that if I kept having my left eye injured I would be blind. Paul once again punched me in it because he felt I didn't do as he told me. My lips were totally deformed and my eye was so battered that it grew three times its size. Anyone who saw me would gasp in horror or cry out in fear.

One particular night Paul wanted to fight me. We argued outside and then I went in the house. A few moments later I heard, "Yeah, well what I do with my girl is none of your business."

"Listen up yo, I just made it my business."

"But yo man, what's it to you?" Paul was yelling loud enough to wake up the neighborhood.

"Grace is a nice girl man, you keep putting your hands on her, just keep it up; three strikes you out! I'm taking her!"

"What? You ain't gonna do nothin'."

There was more cursing, yelling, and then a scuffle. Then the back door slammed. I could hear feet ascending the stairs that led to my room.

My heart was beating so hard I thought I'd die. The footsteps were running full speed upstairs. I heard rapid breathing.

"Grace, it's me, Kathy. Come here, please."

There was more rapid breathing. I stepped out of the room. She was bent over holding her chest, obviously out of breath.

"What's going on out there? Who was that outside taking up for me? Do I know him?"

"Yeah, he's our neighbor. The one who always says 'hi' to you and me when we pass by. But listen, Paul is mad! Bill is gonna take him for a walk to cool him off but stay cool tonight. Don't feed his anger. Let him talk. Don't say a word!"

"Yeah, all right."

I knew it didn't matter if I said something or not. Kathy ran downstairs. I heard the door slam. There were more voices and then silence.

That night Kathy and Bill sat around with Paul and me. They kept their word and didn't leave me alone with Paul. Tyrone slept through the whole episode. I was very thankful. That night Paul threw a lot of questions at me.

"Who is this guy next door who's taking up for you, huh, huh?" He was stumbling around, obviously drunk.

"I don't know him, really. I just see him hanging out with the guys in the yard next door. Just hi and bye is the only conversation we ever had."

"Shut up! Shut up now! You think I'm stupid?!"

"No," I said.

"What? What ya say? You think I'm stupid?"

"No, I don't think ..."

"That's right, you don't think. No, you don't."

I stayed quiet.

"You messing with him? Something going on!"

"No."

"No?! No?! Then why is he taking up for you?"

"I don't know."

"I do! Oh yeah, yeah, okay. I see now, I see now."

"See what, Paul?" I remained amazingly calm.

"Uh-huh, I'm in Brooklyn," he said turning to Bill and Kathy, "I'm in Brooklyn and this b----goes next door and messes around on me."

I remained silent.

"See, lookie there. She's all quiet cause she knows it's true! Huh?" He whirled around to me. "Ain't that right?"

"No."

He leaned his face in close to mine. His eyes were so red, and his breath was hot and reeking of liquor. I screwed up my nose and turned my head.

"Huh, what's up? Tell me the truth!"

Bill leaned forward. "Paul, let it go man. Grace ain't doing nothing. Grace and that baby stay upstairs the whole weekend. She ain't doing nothing man." Paul stood up and raised his hand as if to strike me. I immediately raised mine to block off any offensive blows. Bill jumped up. "Chill! Paul man, chill! Grace ain't doing nothing man!" Paul hesitated then lowered his hands and I lowered mine. His eyes never left my face.

The following night we had a special visitor. His presence didn't evoke a good atmosphere, but it caused a stirring up of violence that would set off a change of events. Bill and his friend from across the street decided to buy some 40-oz. beers, junk food, and play some music so we could have a get-together. I wasn't too keen because it usually turned violent. But I felt a little safe because Bill's friend was a pretty big guy and often he'd come to my defense. Besides, he'd brought a couple of his friends, so I'd eased back.

I had just given Tyrone a bath and was feeding him. He was drifting off to sleep. Then I heard a familiar voice from the previous night. He was greeting everyone and introducing his cousin. It was obvious by his laughing and blending in with other voices that he was very well known. I laid Tyrone down. My curiosity got the best of me, so I tiptoed downstairs and made myself at home in the living room. Kathy entered in from the kitchen. She caught sight of me sitting there.

"Hey Grace! I didn't see ya there. Come on in the kitchen and fix yourself something to drink." I smiled at her and shook my head. "Come on, girl, get something to eat then." She was very drunk. Kathy spilled some of her drink. She disappeared back in the kitchen. There were a lot of people in there, but I dared not enter.

"Grace is in the living room," Kathy spoke out. I guessed that she was talking to Bill but she might as well have been speaking to everyone. "I tried to get her to come in but she just kept shaking her head," she continued. *Thanks a lot Kathy.*

Then a tall, dark handsome, slim guy entered the living room. He sat across the room on a couch that was against the wall.

"What's up, Grace? How ya doing?"

I knew in an instant who he was. I heard a friend call him one time.

"Hi, John," I replied, smiling.

"Traces of Color"

John Sultan was a bold one. He plopped himself down and started talking to me. Eventually, so did his cousin, Larry. They were pretty nice people. The three of us began laughing and talking about our families. I felt very comfortable around them. Paul came in and spoiled the show. He flopped down next to me, spilled some liquor on me, and put his heavy log of an arm around me. I was very embarrassed. "Oh, I'm sorry baby, I spilled some of my drink on you." He pulled me to him and kissed my cheek. "Gimme a kiss."

I leaned over to give him a quick peck on the lips. John never missed a beat. He sat back and smiled. His eyes told me he wasn't buying it.

Paul kept putting it on. "I love this girl here! Yup! This is my baby right here! Gimme some sugar baby." I jumped up and went upstairs. I really hated Paul.

Larry came upstairs and asked if he could watch TV with me. We both sat watching television. Cursing, arguing, laughing, loud talking escalated downstairs, but Larry kept me company.

Then Paul came upstairs, drunker than before. He halted at my room door and looked at Larry. Tyrone had awakened a few minutes earlier and was sitting between us babbling. Paul asked Larry to leave; he wanted to talk to me. I had a plan. The night before I had planted a butcher knife under my bed. I'd said that if Paul hit me again I would kill him while he slept. I had Mrs. Jacobs promise me she would come for Tyrone. Larry leaned over and whispered, "Is he gonna hit you?"

"Yes, but I'm ready for him," I replied.

"Yo," Paul interrupted. "What you asking her anything for?" He spoke in a drunken slur.

"Shut up! Shut up! Alcoholic! I'm tired of you!" I cried. "I'm going to kill you, you watch!" I began yelling and screaming. Paul lunged at me. I shifted Tyrone on the couch so that he wound up in Larry's arms. I kicked Paul in his leg. He stumbled and fell onto my bed. In an instant I grabbed hold of an empty beer bottle I'd left sitting on my dresser for such a time as this. I brought it down forcefully on his skull. Blood began to gush out of his head. The beer bottle had broken and made two small cuts on my hand. Paul collapsed on my bed, moaning and holding his head. Larry jumped up and began pushing me toward the door. I stood there, dripping with blood. Paul was slowly rising off the bed. He spoke piercing words that came out slowly. I could see that he was hurting and wanted to inflict the same punishment. Larry kept shoving me toward the door. He laid Tyrone in the crib. Tyrone was about eight or nine months and had pulled himself. He was reaching for me, crying and babbling da-da. I reached for him but Larry pushed me away. By then Paul was on his feet still speaking vengeance. "I'm gonna kill you, you so-and-so. You gonna regret what you just did."

"Run! Grace run," Larry screamed.

Paul was heading toward the door but Larry's tall frame blocked him in the room. "Run! Grace Run!" Larry screamed.

I turned and fled down the stairs. Kathy and Bill grabbed me and threw me in their room. Kathy locked the door. I hastily tried to tell Bill that Tyrone was upstairs alone with Paul. "Don't worry about that; he's safe, you're not if you don't stay out of sight! Now stay in here." He slammed the door and Kathy locked it. It was dark in their room but I could see the outline of her eyes in the darkness. It covered us like a blanket. I heard Paul and Larry running down the stairs.

"Bill, Bill," Paul was yelling, "Where's Grace? Where's Grace?"

"Paul, what's going on? I just came in from outside. I tried to stop Grace but she ran off down the street," Bill said.

"Yo Bill, don't play with me man!"

"I'm not; she's gone!"

"Where she ran off to?"

"Toward Straightpath."

John entered the dialogue.

"What happened to Grace?"

"Paul was trying to fight her and she ran off somewhere," Larry offered. "I told her to run."

"What? Did you stab her? Did you?" John pressed.

"No! I didn't stab her. She hit me in my head. That so-and-so is crazy!" Paul screamed.

There was a scuffle, loud voices and yelling. Then silence returned. Kathy and I continued to lean against the door. Then we let out a breath.

"Kathy," I said, "I'm dead. You have to help get me out here."

"Keep your voice down," Kathy warned. "Paul could be around still."

The back door opened up. There was a knock at the bedroom door. "It's me, Bill." Kathy opened the door.

"Paul is gone. I gave him some money and he's heading off to Brooklyn in a few. Grace, come out, he's gone."

I was shaking. I ran upstairs to check on Tyrone. He was asleep in the crib, snoring, with his butt hunched up in the air. I was glad to see that he was okay. I went into my bedroom and sat on my bed. I was scared, alone, and wanted out of this mess. For the first time in years I prayed and asked the Lord for help. He heard.

Chapter 7

Loose Ends

For weeks, Paul stayed in Brooklyn. John had moved in with Larry. Bill needed the rent money, so John asked him if he was willing to rent him and his cousin the empty room in the back. John threw some money at him. Bill grabbed the hook and took the bait. I was nervous but glad because maybe Paul would act right with John staying in the house.

This move brought John and me closer. John loved Tyrone. He would carry Tyrone around and play with him for hours when I was too tired and would take Tyrone out for walks and to the studio where he would cut a record. John was a gifted rap artist. One day we went to his friend's studio, which was inside his basement. The studio belonged to Thomas Brown. He let me push buttons and try to make up my own beats. It was fun.

I shared my inward thoughts with John one day. I told him how I wanted out of my relationship with Paul but was afraid he would never let me go. John said that if I wanted Paul to leave me alone, he would help me. I doubted it because Paul was savage. John, on the other hand, was comical and friendly. I never saw him angry. However, John's Jekyll was no match for Paul's Hyde. John told me if I dumped Paul and took him I'd never have to worry again. I didn't say anything, but I did think about it.

Weeks had turned into months and I didn't hear from Paul. I was free! I began to drink again, run the streets, and hang-out with Mrs. Jacobs' niece, Doris, who lived down the street. We went to clubs, met guys and became drinking pals.

John baby-sat Tyrone whenever I wanted to go out. He was always at the house watching TV or heading for the studio. He loved Tyrone's company. But John didn't have a job. He said that he had some money in the bank from working with some well-known people. I was ecstatic. I asked him why he didn't buy a house; it was better than renting a room. He simply wanted to save for his future, establish a business, get married, and have a family. That all cost money.

So John and I started seeing each other. I felt I should let Paul know, even though I didn't hear from him for quite some time. Tyrone was one year old. So one day I walked to the pay phone and called Paul. He was happy to hear from me. He told me that he changed. He had given me my space so I could heal and promised never to hit me again. I pushed his words out my mind. I focused on my rehearsed words instead. I told him I didn't want to see him anymore. I was moving on with my life. I was just calling to say good-bye. "So Good-bye, Paul. Oh yeah, I'm seeing John now." There was silence from the other end of the phone.

"Paul, are you there?" More silence. "Hello?"

"Yeah, I'm still here. So you're seeing John now, huh?"

"Uh-Huh."

"Just like that? I knew you were seeing him. I knew it! You lying so and so," he yelled.

"Paul! Let me talk all right!"

"No! You lied."

"No! I didn't," I screamed.

"You know, tell John I'm coming out to Wyandanch with my boys and we are gonna wreck stuff up."

He hung up abruptly. I ran back and begged John not to stay around. But John threw a party that night and invited all his friends. There were loads of booze and food. John set up the speakers in the basement along with heavy stereo equipment. People started flowing in after hearing there was a party. Among the crowd was John's ex-girl friend and her crew. They called themselves the

Deer Park crew. Every single one of them was beautiful. These females were known to sweep into Wyandanch alone and end up with someone else's man, or a mob of guys running behind them.

That night it began to snow. Paul never showed up.

"The Brawl"

The next day snow blanketed the whole community. John and I were knocked out asleep. John was not a drinker. He had scored points with me the night before because even though his ex tried to get him to leave with her, he sent her on her way. We were asleep when I heard a knock at the door. I was up in a flash. I sat there just listening. John began to stir beside me. The pounding on the door continued.

"John, the door!" I said.

"Oh, that must be my mom. She's supposed to come over today," he said.

"No, John! That's not your mom, it's Paul," I said nervously. "You'd better go," I continued. John laughed.

"Go where? I live here. Relax, will you?"

John tried to hold me but I pulled away. We exchanged looks. He smiled.

"Relax, Grace. You're all right. He's not gonna do anything."

I wasn't so sure about that. I got off the bed and got dressed. I gestured for him to get up, too.

"Get up. John, please get up."

"Why?" he asked, not moving an inch.

"Because. I don't want Paul to see us like this. Get dressed. Let me talk to him first. Besides, he may have his boys with him."

"He's crazy. This is my town. I grew up here. He's not stupid enough to come on another man's turf. He'll get killed. I don't care how many guys he's rolling with."

"Well, Paul is crazy," I said. "Now get up!"

John got up and went to answer the door. Kathy and Bill were in a drunken sleep. Then John came back upstairs with Paul right on his heels. Paul looked at the bed. The blankets were crumbled. He was enraged. I looked down. John walked over to the bed, flicked on the TV, pulled the blankets on him, and laid down. My eyes almost popped out. John just didn't get it. I cleared my throat.

"Uh John, please leave so I can talk to Paul."

He got up, grabbed the pillow and blanket, and bumped Paul's arm on his way out. Paul lost his balance but quickly regained it.

"Excuse me," John said sweetly. "My bad."

"Yeah, right," Paul sneered.

After John went downstairs, Paul grabbed my arm.

"So, you are getting down with him just like that."

I tried to free my arm, but couldn't. I told him to let me go. Paul used his pointer finger and began poking it against my forehead.

"You will tell John that it's over and you will take me back. Cause if you don't, I'm gonna hurt you."

He kept poking me on my head, then my face. I was shielding my face with my palms.

"Let me go!" I spat out.

"Make me, you're so tough, make me," Paul challenged.

"I will."

Paul dropped my arm and took off his coat.

"Oh yeah! Let's go then. Let's get it on."

He balled up his fist and took a fighter's stance. I declined because I knew I didn't have a chance. John took the staircase in huge bounds.

"Yo, Paul, step now!" he demanded.

"John, no," I objected.

"No, Paul step. Take the stairs or I'll help you. You're out of here."

"Naw, Grace, who's it gonna be, me or him?" Paul asked with a stupid smirk on his face.

I looked at Paul then John. I ran to John. Paul went to hit me and that was the loose cannon that started a war. John pushed me aside and punched

Paul in the face. Paul swung back, catching John's arm. John sent a mixture of blows to Paul's face and body, then delivered a kick to his gut. Larry ran upstairs to see what was going on. He stood there winking at me. "John is gonna be all right; my cousin is no joke. He doesn't need my help."

John got Paul to the head of the top step. They were both breathing hard. "Now, Paul," John panted, "take the stairs or get flung down the stairs." Paul got away from the hold John had him in and headed for me like a ferocious animal. I let out a yelp and turned to run. Paul was just about to grab me when John snatched him by the back of his collar. Paul reached for my brass lamp on the table. John grabbed it and beat Paul in the head with it. Then John held up Paul's bloody head and put it through my bedroom wall. The crashing, banging, and continuous loud noises brought Bill running upstairs.

"Oh, my God!" Bill screamed. "Look at all this blood and the holes in the wall, man!"

"Yo, Bill, help me out man," Paul pleaded. But Bill looked once and went downstairs.

Paul tried to swing at John's head, but John caught his arm. John threw him on the floor and stomped his arm. I grabbed Tyrone and ran downstairs. Kathy was at the foot of the stairs. "Paul met his match," Kathy whispered.

"No," I whispered back. "He's out matched."

Then it got quiet upstairs. Kathy and I raised our eyebrows and shrugged our shoulders. We crept back up. There was a big hole in my wall. Paul was lying on the bed with his face turned to the side. John was kneeling on Paul's back and Paul's pants were pulled down. John then grabbed Paul's underwear and asked, "Do you want me, Paul? Is that it? I'll do it to you right now in your butt."

"John's gay," I whispered to Kathy.
She nodded rapidly. "I know," she gasped.

Larry snapped his head around at us and put a finger to his mouth, signaling for us to be quiet. Larry was quiet, too!

"Come on Paul, you know you want me." John started pulling Paul's underwear down and unzipped his pants.

"No," Paul screamed. "Please, no. Don't do it! Don't do it!"

"What?" John asked slyly. "Don't what?"

"Don't do it man! Please don't." Paul began to sob. His sobbing turned to a wail.

"How does it feel, Paul?" John asked. "You beat on women, make them cry, humiliated them. How does it feel to be humiliated? I warned you, didn't I?"

"Yes, yes" Paul continued to sob. "Yes, yes you warned me."

"Now, I tell you what. I'm gonna let you off the hook, okay? Take the stairs."

"Al – all right."

John got up and re-zipped his pants. He gave Paul a shove.

"Yo man, look at you. Your draws' down; you a mess. Get up and fix yourself like a good little boy."

Paul jumped up and pulled his pants up. He gathered up his coat and put on one of his shoes that had come off during the fight.

"I'm sorry man," Paul offered his hand to John.

"Never mind that, just leave." As Paul was about to leave he turned toward me. By now Kathy and I were standing huddled together in the corner by the steps.

"Grace," he croaked, "I'm sorry."

I looked down. I didn't trust him.

"Enough of that, leave now," John commanded.

He walked up beside Paul with a big smile on his face.

"You know what?" Paul started and took a swing at John. John, as quick as a flash, scooped up Paul and threw him down the stairs. Kathy and I stood there, our mouths agape.

Paul's body flew down the stairs. John ran down the rest of the way and kicked Paul in the head with his steel toe boots. I begged John to stop. He did. When Bill called the police, they came and removed Paul from the property. I didn't see Paul for several years after that.

"A Few More Stains"

After Kathy and Bill broke up, he moved down South, and Kathy moved to Brooklyn. John and I moved into his mom's house because the house where we lived was condemned. I was a few months pregnant with John, Jr. I didn't want to live with John's mom or family. I wanted my own place, but John never kept a job. He wanted to go into the studio constantly. Work was not important to him.

Larry, on the other hand, was a very hard worker who made $800-$900 a week. After two or three months we saved several thousand dollars. We found a three-bedroom high ranch house. The landlord let us move in right away. We paid two months security and a month's rent. A month later the landlord converted the lower level of the house into a two-bedroom apartment.

When I heard that Chris, my friend from high school, and her sister, Leslie, were looking for a place, I got in touch with them. They moved in to the two-bedroom apartment, but didn't stay long.

On March 22, 1991 I gave birth to John, Jr. Larry went his own way. John, the kids, and I returned his mom's house. John's mom, Mrs. Sultan, gave us the downstairs apartment. A month later I was pregnant again, but John and I weren't getting along. John never put his hands on me, but he was lazy and a big dreamer. Although I encouraged him to pursue a career in the music world, he needed a job! Love couldn't pay the bills, but John refused to work. Mrs. Sultan argued with her son constantly.

John had a sister named Terry. She never minded her business and had a nasty attitude. On good days I would talk to her for hours. She was very good with the kids and would baby-sit for me. On bad days she was a hellcat. John and I erupted in one of those arguments one day. I wanted to get married, and he didn't. He kept telling me how people he knew got divorced as quickly as they got married. Eventually, we went to the justice of the peace and were married. My cousin Doris was my witness. When the judge asked whether anyone objected to the marriage, my five-month old son said, "I." We all laughed. I wished I had looked to that moment as a sign.

So John and I got married. I didn't experience any of the physical abuse I had endured with Paul, but I experienced a lot of heartache, tears, and sorrow. Occasionally there were spurts of happiness.

There were times when I would leave early in the morning to look for work. When I returned home around 2:00 p.m. or later, John would still be in bed. The kids would greet me at the door saying, "Mommy, I'm hungry. Mommy, we didn't eat," or "Mommy, Daddy wouldn't listen to us, he's just sleeping."

I had another bone to pick with John. He would leave in the evening and return home at midnight, or days later. When questioned, he would claim that he wasn't the driver and therefore had no control over what time he'd return.

Chapter 8

A Pattern of Dreams

During that time a divine gift that I had neglected began to manifest. It was the gift of dreams. I began to notice a pattern that these dreams came true.

I shared with John one day that our marriage was coming to an end, and that a woman was going to be the one who would help end it. John quickly denied it. I told him not to get nervous just yet for this young lady wasn't in the picture yet. I even went on to describe how she looked, and where the incident would take place. I told him everything but the girl's name. That I didn't know. John immediately wanted to admit me to the loony bin.

Night after night, I had more and more dreams. Some I couldn't describe, some I couldn't remember, and others scared me. In one dream,

I was in a church and a man was in the pulpit. Later, I discovered that it wasn't a man at all, but a vampire or demon of some sort. He and other demons started grabbing, pulling, and even trying to lie with me. I woke up with a start. I was terrified. When I was fully awake, I still felt those hands pulling at my body.

I began to sleep with my kids every night. Often my son John would be asleep in his crib, and then all of a sudden I would see the crib move from against the wall to the middle of the floor, and back again. I thought I was losing my mind. John, by now, had stopped coming home for days. He didn't even call or stop by to see us.

One day I was downstairs playing with my boys. Tyrone was about three, John was one, and Thomas was a few months old. I heard a knock upstairs at the front door. Terry came down from the top-level to answer it. I heard her say, "Shut up, John!"

John came downstairs. He didn't say a word to me. Neither did he look at me. I didn't say anything to him either. I went on playing with the kids as if he wasn't there. I'd learned to do this well from living with Paul. After he came out of my bedroom he spoke to me.

"Hey Grace, how ya doing?"

"Hey, yourself. I'm fine."

"Listen, you need anything?"

"No."

"Have food for yourself?"

"Yup, plenty."

"What ya been doing?"

I spread my hands and pointed them at the kids.

"Do the boys need anything?"

"Thomas needs pampers."

"You all right?"

"Yup."

"Well, okay. I'll be back, all right?"

"Uh-huh."

"Do you want me to buy Thomas the box or the bag?"

I shrugged my shoulders.

"Whatever. Do what you wanna do. You been doing it anyhow."

"What's that supposed to mean?"

"Nothing. Nothing at all."

He turned and left. I continued to play with the boys. About an hour later, John returned. He gave me a box of diapers then left. I kept getting the urge to pursue him. But I tried to ignore it. The more I ignored it the worse it got. I couldn't keep still, so I leaped up the stairs, opened the door, and went outside. John was about to pull off. He didn't see me in the doorway, but I saw him. Someone was with him, but I couldn't make out her face. I jogged up to the car to have a closer look. That's when John noticed me. He hadn't started the engine yet so I knew he couldn't speed away. He rolled down his window. He looked nervous but didn't say a word.

Once I got to the window, I leaned over to my left to have a closer look at the passenger. She leaned to her left to look at me. John sat there looking at me. Once I caught sight of her face, I knew in an instant who she was. It was the girl from my dreams! John never said anything to defend himself when I asked him what was going on. He remained silent. I didn't bust out his window, I didn't curse him, I didn't slash his tires, or punch the girl in the face. I just smiled, waved him on, and said, "Oh yeah, John, remember my dream?"

"Huh, what?"

"My dream John, remember?"

"What dream, Grace?" He was losing patience.

"Never mind," I said, "you can go."

As I turned and headed toward the house John drove away. A month later we split up for good. I was alone with three children to care for. I didn't feel happy and I didn't feel sad. I was still on welfare. I got up each morning before my kids. Every first of the month when I got that check I spent the money on my kids. I paid rent, bills and at times would buy something for myself.

I was once again free.

Chapter 9

The Dark Side

I re-opened a door from my childhood – witchcraft. I called up psychic hotlines. One told me to burn certain colored candles on certain days. I read horoscopes to find out what the outcome of my days ahead would be. I began wearing black from head to toe. I told people I could read their minds, and I was a witch. I no longer had friends.

I took a nursing assistant course at a trade school in Brentwood. There I befriended several people. Two of them were Christians, but the one with whom I was tight, wasn't. Her name was Constance Moyer. Constance and I began to hang out a lot. She was Muslim and could speak Arabic and Spanish. Constance was out-going, friendly, and very funny. My boys loved her. She had tried to set me up with a guy who was incarcerated. I didn't care very much for him. But I sent him magazines, letters, and food. I also visited him. He wasn't what I was looking for.

The dreams I was having were getting worse. I shared with Constance one day in class how I dreamed I was sitting in a tall tree talking to a guy. The tree was on a corner. Lots of cops were going by. I described the guy to her. She then broke into a big smile. "You just described my best friend," she told me. "I used to climb that tree and talk to him. The tree is in a drug-infested area that is heavily patrolled by cops," she explained.

"It was you," I said excitedly. "Why did I see me?"

"Maybe because we are close or something." Constance shrugged.

The dreams kept coming and I kept telling them. Veronica, who was also a classmate, and a guy named Bobby, were always talking about God. Veronica was also very spiritual. She was into the Holy Spirit and gifts of the Holy Spirit. I was intrigued by her, but not enough to make me hungry. What drew my attention was when she said she saw angels. She said she saw them as lights. I found that hard to believe. She also told me that the Lord spoke to her. That made me move my seat. I often felt she was a lunatic. Bobby said he was a minister. He smoked more cigarettes than a chimney. But he talked about the Lord constantly. I never looked to him as being a lunatic, but cool. After our course was over, he gave me his phone number. Veronica gave me hers, too.

I started reading a lot of books by Anne Rice. I would fall asleep with my face still on the page I was reading. I couldn't take the nightmares anymore and was afraid to go to sleep. I began to sleep with the lights on.

I tried to pray, but a voice kept telling me I was wasting my time. "God doesn't love you," it taunted. "He doesn't want you back." "How many times have you messed up; how many times have you gone back?" I listened to the voice. It was true. I had messed up so many times that I felt I could never return. I was growing more tired every day from lack of sleep. I lost a lot of weight and became forgetful. I even forgot my own name. I started practicing palmistry and reading tea leaves. One day, out of desperation, I called Bobby. I told him about all the things I was involved in. Bobby listened for a long time. He didn't interrupt me. After letting me ramble on, I gave him the floor. He told me that Jesus loved me, and that I could come home and be saved again. He also said that my sprit was being tormented by demons. I could call upon the angels of the Lord for help, repent, and tell the Lord I was sorry. Before hanging up, he gave me a prayer to say every night. I wrote it down. He also told me to keep my radio tuned to a Christian station.

I thanked him and hung up. I didn't run by my bedside right away and do as he told me. It was a struggle. Before going to bed I threw away all the horoscope books and candles. I then knelt down and prayed the prayer he gave me. I don't know when I fell asleep but when I woke up, it felt like a new morning. I was so overjoyed. I did not have one nightmare. For a week I slept each night like a baby. I then began praying for a husband. I asked the Lord to send me someone who would love me more than I loved him. I asked the Lord for this person to make a commitment to me. I was tired of the men I had been getting involved with. They were leaving me, but my family size kept growing. That night I had a dream. I was lying in bed sleeping. I saw a little girl between a man and me. I didn't see this man's face, just his body, and I heard his voice.

Chapter 9

A Hopeful Corner

One year later, as I was in the kitchen washing dishes, I felt an urge to look out the window. There wasn't anything out of the ordinary going on out there, just a bunch of guys I knew hanging out at the corner house, smoking weed. But there was one who stood out from the rest. He was talking, laughing, and smoking weed, too. I went outside to investigate him. I started throwing a ball to my boys. We were laughing, rolling around, and chasing each other. The interesting guy was staring at me. Over the next couple of days I repeated this scene. He would spot me coming, run outside, sit on his friend's step, and greet me. I'd say, "Hi," and keep on going. I would be about half a block up just to find him closer to the street, standing and staring at me. I would turn around smile and keep going.

On one occasion I decided to invite myself into the group. I had just bought my son John, Jr. a bicycle. Tyrone had one and had broken his. Thomas was throwing a tantrum because he wanted one, too. I couldn't afford another bike but promised him that in a few weeks I would buy him one.

I walked across the street to where the guys were standing. Terry and her younger brother decided to come, too. John, Jr. was riding his bike, falling down, and getting up. Even though he was getting all scuffed up, he had the biggest smile on his face. Vinny and Calvin came over to speak to me and that brought mystery man over too. He was a pretty handsome man, not too tall, and buffed. He looked like a player, but was very friendly. He played with my kids and my kids played back with him.

"You got some cute kids, Grace," he said.

"Excuse me, but what is your name?"

"Oh, I'm sorry. My name's David."

There weren't sparks flying between us. They were flying only from David's end. Every day after that, he made it his business to speak to me.

I remember going to the ice cream truck to buy my kids some ice cream. David was standing in Calvin and Vinny's front yard about to smoke an L. (weed). His eyes were already redder than a fire truck. He could hardly stand up! "You got it going on," he was saying. "Your hair so long and nice, too."

I turned around and looked at him. He showed me all his teeth. I smirked back at him.

"Thank you but this hair is a weave," I said sweetly.

David didn't bat an eye or skip a beat.

"Yeah well, you still look good!"

I was lost for words. I looked over at Alphonso who was also there listening to the whole conversation.

"I saw you the other day. You was standing there in the living room and your hair was standing on top of your head. But I didn't mind standing there watching you."

I could have blasted Mrs. Sultan for not putting up some curtains in her living room.

"You shouldn't be looking in people's windows. What are you, a peeping Tom?"

"Nope. But I didn't mind peeping at you."

Everyone was hearing the conversation and laughing. About a few weeks after that we began seeing each other. I thought David would be out the door once we slept together. But he always came back. He brought my son Thomas a bicycle the first week we went out. Thomas didn't like David at all! But after that gift, they became the best of friends. David had a good paying job. Around the second week of our relationship, I didn't have money to buy sneakers for John and

Thomas. On his payday, he spent over one hundred dollars on the two of them. I went off on him, but he just laughed. I told him he could have bought them cheaper sneakers. He replied, "As long as I'm around, they're not wearing cheap sneakers." Every time he came over he never came empty handed. He brought me flowers, food for the house and took us out to eat every Friday. The boys loved him and I liked him, but I didn't want to get my hopes too high.

Around the second or third week of our relationship, he asked me to marry him. I said yes, even though I still was married to John.

Chapter 10

Removing the Old

In September of 1993, I became pregnant and broke the news to David. He scooped me up and kissed me. "I love you," he exclaimed. David would run out no matter how late it was to feed my food cravings.

One particular day he was very upset.

"What is it?" I asked.

"My mom is over at the house talking about Jesus."

"Maybe the Lord is calling you to be saved, David."

"What do you mean?"

I told him about salvation, sin, and the love of Jesus Christ, although I wasn't living right myself.

The following week David's friend, an ordained minister, invited David to hear him preach. Later on that evening David returned from the church service. His eyes were red, and he had tears flowing down his cheeks.

"What's wrong David?" I asked.

"I accepted Jesus Christ as my Savior," is all he said.

I said, "Oh."

We didn't talk any more about it. He refused to have any sexual relationship with me, he stopped smoking weed and cigarettes, and he stopped hanging out with his friends. I, on the other hand, chose to remain an outsider looking in on the body of Christ. David began reading his Bible and was always asking me questions on scriptures he didn't understand. I patiently answered. David was so overjoyed at being saved. He rambled on about his new love. I felt a little jealous but I couldn't get myself to surrender all to the Lord just yet.

David was always a gentleman. I couldn't take it. I felt smothered. I tried to get him to go out and do other things but he refused. "You are the person I want to be with, not my friends," he insisted.

His mother and I got along fine at first. She didn't mind that I had three children, but she minded the fact that I was still married to John and was seeing her son. She began to become distant. I was pregnant with her grandchild and that made things even worse. She had told people that her son could go a lot further without me, and would even be better off without me. I expected better from her.

In 1993, David spent Christmas with the kids and me. In January, I moved from Mrs. Sultan's house into a homeless shelter because I had been given an ultimatum: either let David go, or be with him and live in a shelter. I chose David and left.

Chapter 11

Rounding the Corners

I was four months pregnant, with three children, and nowhere to go. I couldn't return to Mrs. Jacobs because she had a full house. I turned to social services for help. They sent the kids and me to a homeless shelter in Bellport, Long Island. It was like being on a remote island. The shelter was nice, but it felt like prison. We had curfews. We were allowed to receive phone calls in our apartments, but couldn't make outside calls from there. We had to go to pay phones. We had twenty-four hour security. There were police officers who patrolled the premises constantly. They were also very nice. The case workers did all they could to be helpful. They worked on the facility also. They kept us updated on permanent housing options and helped us get established once we were outside again. They made sure we were comfortable (but not too comfortable). The kids and I were sharing a one-bedroom apartment. I didn't have a television but I had brought my radio. I tuned in to Family Radio, which I played day and night. While my boys slept I got on my hands and knees and prayed for the Lord to help us find a place to live.

I called David's mom and gave her the phone number to my apartment. She promised to give it to David, and she did. David called me on his lunch breaks and after he got home. He even walked to pay phones late at night to call me, but it was useless because we weren't allowed phone calls after a certain time.

Then one day, during a blizzard when everyone was told to stay home, I received a call from the office. I had a visitor. I got the boys dressed. We had to put on layers of clothing. My pre-pregnancy weight was one hundred and twenty-three pounds, but I had ballooned to one hundred seventy pounds. I put on what I could and went to the front office. It was David! He had taken a train then a cab to see me. He had even brought a 19" inch color television, clothes, and a dozen white roses.

David began working overtime and was saving every dime he made. He found a three-bedroom apartment in Wyandanch for $950.00 a month. The landlord wanted one month's rent and one month's security, plus David had to pay the real estate agent $950.00. I felt hopeless. I told David it would take an eternity. But he never gave up.

He kept on saving his money. I kept doing what I did best, complaining.

During this period there was a childhood demon who came to oppress me. His name was suicide. I couldn't entertain him because I was carrying another life at the time. I told him to come back another time. David paid for the place in four months. In a few days we would move into a three-bedroom apartment.

The day the kids and I left the shelter and moved into the apartment, David wasn't there when we arrived. He was at work. He had informed the tenants downstairs that I was moving in. There was a young lady who was waiting at the front door for me.

She introduced herself. I chose not to socialize then because I was upset with the house's outward appearance. The door was coming off its hinges, the yard had patches of grass, and the rest of it was dirt where grass should have been. There was a pack of wild dogs running around terrorizing other dogs. These dogs chose to make our backyard their habitation. The house's paint was peeling very badly. The house looked like it should have been condemned.

That night David and I had our first argument. I was complaining and David tried continually to console me. He kept apologizing about the house. Eventually, I calmed down and thanked him. The argument was over.

Chapter 12

Coming Clean

In June of 1994, I gave birth to my fourth son, David Dyer, III. Things were going fine for David and me. The kids were getting older and David had a great job.

One day I dreamed I was standing before the throne of God. My head was hung down and my hands hung limply by my sides. No one spoke to me. I sensed people standing all around me, but no one spoke. Then all of a sudden I was standing in a strange place. It was dull, gloomy and lifeless. There were tiny insects bumping against my arm. I kept brushing them off. I was very frightened. I looked up and saw a tunnel of pure darkness. I knew without a doubt it was an entrance to hell. I looked up and cried out with a loud voice, "You don't want me to go in there, do you?" I heard the Lord say, "You are at the gate, turn around!" I woke up with a start. I was so glad it was just a dream. In that dream every single one of my five senses was fully alert and active.

I called David at his job. I told him what happened. He tried to reassure me. It didn't work. I then made the decision to go back to church. I started attending David's god-father's church.

Jesus re-instated my position in His body. I began studying the Bible, teaching the Word, and telling anyone who would listen about Jesus Christ and His precious gift of salvation. David, on the other hand, stopped going to church and reading the Word of God. He was in a backslidden state.

I grew closer and closer to God. I began to pray at twelve o'clock. I would pray, read the Bible, and sing songs unto the Lord every day for one hour. There would be times David and I would settle down together to watch a movie and just like a timer going off on the inside of me I would jump up without even hesitating, go to my bedroom, shut the door, get on my knees and pray. David never could understand this new thing with God and me.

One day, after my prayer hour, I climbed into my bed and went to sleep. I don't know how long I was sleeping. A voice was teaching me about Moses. I began to cry out that it was too much to remember it all. But the voice said in a whisper, "You will when it's time." Then it faded away.

I jumped up and ran down the hallway into the living room. When I told David my experience he looked at me.

"What did he look like Grace?" David asked.

"I didn't see His face, I just heard his voice."

"What did it sound like?"

The question stumped me.

"He sounded like the wind. No wait, a breeze, no, like water." I was puzzled.

"Oh," was all he said. He patted my hand.

I knew what I heard. It had to be the Holy Spirit! His voice sounded like those things. David continued watching his show. I turned and stomped back to my room. I knew I heard the voice of God.

But that visitation wasn't the end; I remember receiving a visitation from Jesus Christ. He took me into heaven and told me things that I was to do here on earth. I remember telling Jesus that I couldn't do the job and that I wasn't going to remember. But Jesus kept telling me that I would make it, and He loved me. I felt love and happiness. I didn't want to come back to earth.

I continued to listen to Family Radio. I began listening to a particular minister. He was telling people that the world was coming to an end in 1994. I liked his teaching ministry at the time. I ran out and bought his book. I was running around telling people to repent for Jesus was coming on September 6, 1994. Everyone really thought I was nuts. David became frantic because he didn't know if he was really saved or not, so just to be safe, he re-committed himself to Christ.

On September 4, 1994, I had another dream. In the dream I was looking out the window. I wasn't alone. There were two people standing next to me. We were looking down at the earth. People in the dream were running around. There were major car accidents, night had fallen, the moon turned to blood, and there were lots of fighting, crying, hollering, and looting. I heard the Lord say, "I'm not coming September 6th. Before I do, the world is going to be in chaos." I woke up. I told David my dream. My mind was put at ease but David's wasn't.

On September 6, 1994 the world continued on just as God had said.

Chapter 13

A New Friend

David and I got married on September 21, 1996. Times were rough for us. More times than I can remember, we barely had enough food or clothes, but I prayed about any and everything.

One cold winter morning, while the kids were still sleeping, I waited for David to return from his night job at Toys "R" Us. I expected him within a few hours. I had given him two dollars in food stamps to get a loaf of bread. We were going to eat peanut butter and jelly sandwiches. As I laid in bed waiting for David to come in, I began to talk with Jesus. I told Him all about my troubles. Then I heard the kids stirring around in the other room, so I decided to get up, too. As I left the bedroom and entered the living room I heard a strange noise at the front door. Curious, I peeked out the front door just to find two grocery bags hanging on the front door knob. I took them inside and placed them on the table. Inside were five loaves or more of bread and Bogali pizza crusts and sauce. I cried out, "Praise the Lord!" That brought the kids running. "What, Mommy?" They yelled. I told them God blessed us with food. They danced. At that time, I was pregnant with my daughter Faith.

Chapter 14

Fitting it All Together

I befriended the owner of the Genesis Christian Bookstore that was right down the street from me. We would talk about the Lord, I would buy a book or two, and leave. One particular day when I came in, there was another woman there, too. She had her back to me so I couldn't see her face. I was browsing through some books and found a few I was interested in. I brought them to the counter, only to find the woman there, too. The owner was on the phone with a customer so the woman, who introduced herself as Yvonne, and I engaged in a conversation about one of the books. After the owner got off the phone, she rang up the books. She told me to wait; she would take me home. I refused the offer. I tried to open the door but it wouldn't open. The other customer then said, "I'll take you home." I objected again, and kept trying to open the door.

"Okay. I'll be obedient. You can take me home."
I tried the door again and it opened right up. The
lady and I left the store.

When we arrived at my home, we sat in the
car for four or five hours just talking. She told me
about her marriage, family and enemies. It wasn't
the first two things she mentioned that got my
attention, but the last one. She told me that her
enemies were witches and they worked witchcraft
against her. I was intrigued. I told her I had
studied witchcraft when I was younger and had
even thought about becoming one. I thanked God
that I met Jesus first. I liked Yvonne and I felt she
had a lot of information about life. I was willing
to learn. She invited me to attend church with
her. So on Friday night we went together. The
preacher spoke, and before he closed the service,
he called people up to the altar.

He told them how Jesus was straightening out
whatever ailed them. I turned to Yvonne and
whispered," Why didn't you tell me this man was
a prophet?" Yvonne looked at me and shrugged
her shoulders. "I didn't think you'd come if I told
you," she said. He began walking down the aisle.
He stopped and looked at me. I was scared. I
prayed he wouldn't call me. He did. I went down
the aisle. As soon as I got there I felt light-headed.
I quickly shook myself to clear my head. He began
describing my husband David and how the Lord

was going to use him and bless my family. I thanked the Lord and sat down.

Yvonne and I went everywhere together. She was a great friend, not just to me, but to my whole family. She brought us food whenever we had a need. We visited many churches. Evangelists, prophets and pastors would stop and tell Yvonne what a mighty woman of God she was. I, on the other hand, would get a "God loves you, you are special, or you are a very gifted songstress." I became jealous of Yvonne. But because I heard all these things about her, it made me chase after God. I would come home from church and start bawling.

David would just lie in the bed, look at me and say, "Don't tell me – Yvonne got a word tonight from God and you didn't." That only made me cry harder. I started praying and reading more scriptures. When I started getting called out, the Lord told me He had called me to be a prophetess.

Chapter 15

The Quilt Meets the Comforter

The position of "prophetess" came with a price. Bills piled up, rent couldn't be paid, and David lost his job. I sank into depression. I made up my mind this time. I went to the store and bought sleeping pills and alcohol. David told me he couldn't live without me and wanted to come. I told him no. He had to stay for the kids. David agreed. He decided to leave because he said he couldn't see me kill myself.

When he left the kids were in bed. I got the pill bottle, sat on the couch, and prayed. "Father you are my mother, my friend, my sister, my brother, any thing you need to be." I told Jesus I was depressed, couldn't take it and I wanted to come home. I asked Him to forgive me for what I was about to do. I picked up the bottle. "Boom! Boom! Boom!" went the door.

"Grace, Grace! Open the door! Please open the door!"

I was startled.

"Who is it?" I yelled out.

"It's Yvonne."

"Come in. The door is open."

Yvonne rushed in, hysterical.

"Grace, what's wrong? Something is wrong."

"What do you mean?" I asked calmly.

"Well," she said, "I was on Straightpath and the Lord told me to come to your house. I told the Lord that you weren't there, so I decided to keep driving. But then His voice thundered out "GO NOW!" I whipped that car around, almost got into an accident, and I came here. Now what is going on?"

I told her all I was about to do and how I didn't want to live anymore.

"Gimme those pills," she said and snatched them from me. "Where is David?" she asked.

I told her how David bought some vodka and left.

"He's driving?" she yelped.

"Uh-huh."

"Oh Lord," she prayed, "please watch over David and bring him home safely Lord, please. Grace you're coming to church with me. Get the kids dressed and come on."

I didn't move. David burst through the door.

"Thank God you didn't take those pills. I came back to stop you."

"Yeah! And thank God you're safe, too," Yvonne said.

"Yvonne, I'm not even drunk. I finished the whole bottle, but I'm not drunk!"

That night I went to church with Yvonne. The pastor prayed for me. He said, "God says to tell you this: 'Daughter I love you. You are a good girl.'" I just looked at the preacher. "This is what you said to God: 'You are my mother, my father.'" My mouth fell open. No one heard me say those words but God. Yvonne wasn't even there. That's when I knew God does hear and answer prayer.

Chapter 16

Completing the Quilt

I went into labor on New Year's Eve. David prayed the baby would be born so we could make the newspapers. The hospital was crowded with women who had gone into labor, but after a few hours we were sent home. I returned to the hospital a day later. My labor pains were intensifying. The nurse checked me and said I was only a fingertip dilated. I was upset. I told David to pray that God would speed things up and get this baby out of me. David held my hands and prayed. The nurse tried to make small talk with me.

"What are you having, Grace?" she asked.

"A girl," I panted.

"Oh. Did you have a sonogram?"

"Uh-huh."

"And that's how you know."

"No."

"How do you know?"

"God told me in a dream," I said.

She smirked and told me she didn't want me to be disappointed.

"Don't get your hopes up," she said. "He did tell me," I insisted. I began describing how my daughter would look. I described her hair. I also told the nurse I saw my child in a dream five years ago, sitting between my husband and me. "Tell her David," I said.

David told the nurse it was all true. I explained that my dreams were one of the gifts that God had given me. The nurse just shook her head and left the room. A few hours later I delivered a healthy baby girl. The nurse was baffled.

"How did you know all this, really?" she asked.

"I told you!" I smiled at her.

"You're scaring me," she said and hurried on to the next room.

I named my daughter Faith. After having four boys I felt that's what I needed to have her. Two years later I had a baby boy.

*****

The pastor of the church I was attending put me in charge of a group of unruly children. I told her that I didn't want the job. But she insisted. "Grace, these teenagers like you and I think you will work great with them," she encouraged.

"What do you want me to do?" I asked.

"I want to put you in charge of the choir."

My mouth fell open. There was no way I was going to teach them to sing.

Not long after that conversation, I was appointed choir director. Working with the kids wasn't easy at first, but after a few weeks they were more cooperative. I found out that these kids could really sing. I found songs they would like. I even treated them to donuts and juice. I would sit and talk with the girls and find out what was going on in their lives. They looked forward to seeing me Sunday after Sunday.

The Lord began to open up many doors for me in speaking engagements. I was invited to a church to conduct a women's conference. When visiting pastors heard me speak, they set up dates to have me come to their church to preach. I was excited about all the events that were happening in my life. I finally was having a chance at happiness. I'm not saying that it's perfect but it's definitely worth living.

One day I sat in my bedroom and wrote a song. I sang it to David and asked his opinion of it.

"Where did you hear that? The radio?" he asked.

"No. I made it up," I said.

He didn't believe me. I told him to give me a topic and I'd be back in five minutes with a song. He did. Five minutes later I returned. David was ecstatic.

"You can write? I can't believe it," he cried.

"Do you think I'm good?" I asked.

"Yeah!" he said.

I ran to the room and showed him my notebook that was filled with lyrics. I even showed him a book I was working on, too. I read him some pages. He was so excited. He asked how long I had been a writer. I told him since second grade. My life was filled with poetry, too. But I didn't think I was any good.

Epilogue

David began encouraging me to write. He was the one who suggested that I tell my life story. He told me he would back me up one hundred percent. I prayed and asked God what He thought, and He agreed.

I met a friend who said she had a friend who owned her own publishing company. After a few weeks I called. The publisher encouraged me to write my story. David watched the kids while I sat in my room and began to write. How did I make out? Well, that's another story.

I never knew my biological dad. I don't think about him as much as I used to when I was a little girl. But now, I consider the Lord as my real father. He's always been there for me. He always listens to me, no matter what time it is. He's always protected me from so many dangers.

There is no way I could end this book without expressing my deepest thanks to Him.

I love you Father, because You first loved me.

XXX♥

To obtain additional copies of

The Tattered Quilt

Ask for it at your local bookstore or

Send a check or money order
for $17.50 *($14.99, plus $2.50 s/h)* to:

Word For Word Publishing Co.
c/o Grace Dyer
14 MetroTech Center
Brooklyn, NY 11201

Ask for discounts on multiple copies.